A Study Guide for the
Revised RICA

A Guideline for Reading Instruction in Grades Kindergarten to Eight, and
Preparation Guide for the Revised California RICA™.

Marilyn Dye, M.S.

Aligned with the Revised RICA™ Content Specifications and the *Reading/
Language Arts Framework for California Public Schools, 2007*

Education Resource Publishing
San Diego

Study Guide for the California RICA
By Marilyn Dye, M.S.

Education Resource Publishing
10601-G Tierrasanta Blvd. Suite 260
San Diego, CA 92124
Email: edresource@san.rr.com

Printed in the United States of America

Cover and Book Design by Robin Dye
Copy Editor Robin Richardson

Library of Congress Control Number 2001012345
ISBN-13: 978-0-9841970-0-2

Contents

PREFACE

This guide is designed to be a review of assessments and instructional strategies and activities involved in the effective instruction of reading in Grades K-8. It is intended as an instructional outline for reading and a preparation guide to the revised California RICA™ examination.

In 1996 the ***California Reading Advisory*** stated:

> "As a state, we must not be willing to settle for partial accomplishment of our goals. We must provide a balanced and comprehensive reading and writing program in our schools so that every child will be ensured success as an effective reader, writer, and thinker. This is our goal, this is our mandate, and every possible resource must be directed toward this work. For the children of California to succeed in literacy, the teachers of California must be effective. Parents, community, and the entire state must be part of the effort and must contribute their support to the teachers and children in our schools. We are in this process together, for the children."

The California Reading Initiative was approved by the State Board of Education in September of 1996. As a part of this initiative AB1178 established a new requirement for a preliminary teaching credential - demonstration of knowledge, skill, and ability in reading instruction. The bill provided monies to the Commission on Teacher Credentialing to develop a competency assessment. Competency would be established either through a written examination or an observational assessment. As a result of this law, and because of the critical importance of reading instruction in the classroom, candidates for the Multiple Subject Teaching Credential and Education Specialist Instruction Credential (special education) are required to pass the Reading Instruction Competence Assessment (RICA™). The purpose of the RICA™ is to ensure that prospective teachers have the knowledge and skills to provide effective reading instruction in a balanced, comprehensive program in Grades K - 8. Candidates must take either the RICA™ Written Examination or the RICA™ Video Performance Assessment.

The RICA™ examination includes fifteen areas of reading instructional competencies. These areas are divided into five content domains. Although the examination itself is not divided into the five domains, it includes questions and case studies that require a knowledge and understanding of the content in each of the five domains. This guide outlines the five domains and the knowledge and skills necessary to provide assessment and instruction in these areas.

The RICA™ Written Examination consists of three sections that assess the candidate's knowledge of and ability to apply that knowledge to effective reading instruction:

Focused Educational Problems and Instructional Tasks
This section presents problems and tasks in educational contexts, and requires candidates to (a) consider information about a class, a group of students, an individual student, or an instructional

situation and, (b) devise appropriate instructional strategies or assessment approaches. Each form of the exam includes four focused educational problems and instructional tasks. For Domains 3 and 4, each problem or task requires a one-page written response. For Domains 2 and 5, each problem or task requires a two-page written response.

Case Study

For this section of the exam, candidates receive substantial background information about a student as well as materials that illustrate the student's reading performance. Candidates are asked to assess the student's reading performance, describe appropriate instructional strategies, and explain why these strategies would be effective. Each form of the exam includes one case study. All five of the RICA content domains are addressed. This section requires a four-page written response.

Multiple Choice Questions

On each form of the RICA Written Examination, the case study and the four focused educational problems and tasks are supplemented by approximately 70 multiple-choice items. These include content questions, which directly assess knowledge of reading and reading instruction, as well as contextualized questions that assess the credential candidate's ability to apply specific knowledge, to analyze specific problems, or to carry out specific tasks related to reading instruction. Overall, the multiple-choice questions assess knowledge and skills in the five RICA™ content domains as follows:

Domain 1	14 items
Domain 2	23 items
Domain 3	7 items
Domain 4	16 items
Domain 5	10 items

Candidates are given four hours to complete the exam and are free to spend as much or as little time as they like on either section of the examination. (Information from the RICA™ Registration Bulletin)

HOW TO USE THIS BOOK

The RICA™ is a practical examination designed to assess a beginning teacher's knowledge of assessments, management techniques, strategies, and activities involved in teaching children to read. The questions relate directly to situations the teacher will encounter in the classroom, and the candidate will be expected to demonstrate an understanding of the concepts and strategies needed in the instruction of reading. It is of little value to memorize the definition of terms out of context. The important factor is understanding the concepts. One must have a thorough understanding of reading assessments, how to analyze the assessments, and how to plan instruction based on assessment results. Knowledge of specific activities and strategies used to teach to students' strengths and weaknesses is also necessary.

While studying from this study guide, it is suggested that the candidate have access to the RICA website, www.rica.nesinc.com. This website specifies the skills and knowledge expected of a competent teacher of reading. This study guide is directly aligned with these competencies. The guide expands on the outline and suggests specific assessments and instructional strategies and activities for each competency.

Practice in writing case studies provides excellent preparation for the RICA™. *Case Studies in Preparation for the California Reading Competency Test,* by Joanne Rossi and Beth Schipper, provides an excellent companion to this book and gives a variety of types of cases and supporting worksheets. The scenarios reflect real-world situations that teachers might encounter in the classroom.

For further clarification and expansion on the concepts, strategies, and activities mentioned in this guide, refer to such reading instruction textbooks as *Teaching Reading Source Book,* (2000) by Bill Honig, Linda Diamond, and Linda Gutlohn or Phonics They Use, 5th edition, by Patricia Cunningham. *Phonics They Use* is referred to throughout this study guide and provides candidates with additional activities for reading instruction.

To fully understand California's expectations at each grade level, candidates should be familiar with the *Reading/Language Arts Framework for California Public Schools, K-12* (2007) and the California Content Standards for Reading. This can be accessed through www.gov.edu This website will be helpful not only in studying for the RICA but in planning an instructional program in the classroom.

I hope you will find this study guide helpful. Best of luck in your teaching!

Marilyn

ABOUT THE AUTHOR

Recently retired, Marilyn Dye was a reading specialist for the Chula Vista Elementary School District in Chula Vista, California for twenty years. She has taught reading methodology classes and RICA™ preparation classes for Azusa Pacific University and National University in San Diego. Fifteen years of experience in K-6 classrooms has provided her with practical experience in working with children of all ages in a diverse population. She has been involved with curriculum writing both for the Chula Vista Elementary School District and for National University. She is committed to the development of pre-service teacher preparation in the field of reading instruction.

TEST-TAKING TIPS FOR THE RICA

- Be sure to budget your time. Leave at least an hour at the end for the Case Study.

- There are more Multiple Choice questions in Domains 2 and 5. This should be considered when prioritizing your study time.

- The essay questions are longer for Domains 2 and 5. Keep this in mind when prioritizing your study time.

- The questions have choices A-D, no "all of the above" or "none of the above". Some of them are very lengthy. If you are not sure of the answer, go back and re-read the question and determine exactly what it is asking. <u>Underline the main points of the question.</u> The questions are practical, common sense questions.

- Many students find it helpful to read the essay questions first and then go back and complete the Multiple Choice questions. The content of the Multiple Choice questions can be helpful in answering the essay questions. Often a sentence from a multiple choice question can be used as an introductory sentence for the essay. The terminology used in the Multiple Choice questions can be useful in formulating ideas for the essay.

- When answering, do not limit yourself to something you have read in a book or learned in a methodology class. If you have had experience as an aide, a parent volunteer in a classroom, helping your own child with their schoolwork, or even watching Sesame Street or some other educational program with your child, all of these experiences will give you practical knowledge from which to draw. Draw on things you remember your own child's teacher using in the classroom.

- Be sure that your answer matches the prompt they have given you or the question they have asked

- If you are "stuck" on one question, move on and come back to it later.

- These two websites are good websites to use for practicing sample questions: www.rica.nesinc.com and http://gsep.pepperdine.edu/ricatesting.

- On the essays you will be asked to analyze information they provide and <u>identify the needs</u> of either a class or a student. After identifying the needs you will need to identify <u>instructional strategies , activities, and interventions to meet the need</u>. You then need to tell <u>why</u> you chose those particular interventions for the identified need. Remember AIR (analyze

Assessments, describe Interventions, and give Rationale.)

- For the Case Study you will be given assessments, data, anecdotal records surveys, etc. to analyze and then asked to identify a strength **or** a need of a student. Your task is to 1) <u>identify the strength or need</u>, 2) tell some <u>strategies or activities</u> that you would use to instruct, and 3) tell <u>why</u> you chose those particular strategies or activities. **Be sure your strategies and activities match the identified needs .** (i.e. If the identified need is in Phonemic Awareness, don't give strategies that instruct in Concepts of Print.)

- When answering your written questions it is important that you be specific and give examples of how you would instruct. Do not use generalizations or assume they will know what you are talking about – be explicit. **Write your explanation of activities as if you were leaving plans for a substitute. Be sure your activity relates to the specific skill you are teaching.**

- One of the biggest obstacles many have to overcome is test anxiety. Being prepared is the first step in alleviating anxiety. Study hard and then relax the night before the test. Last minute "cramming" can be confusing and often does more harm than good. Get plenty of sleep. Leave your personal problems, concerns, and distractions out in the hallway and focus on the exam. The most important thing is to believe in yourself. Know that you have the knowledge and the ability to do well on the RICA

INSTRUCTIONAL DOMAINS FOR

THE RICA

DOMAIN 1
Assessment and Planning Instruction

DOMAIN 2
Word Analysis

DOMAIN 3
Fluency

DOMAIN 4
Vocabulary, Academic Language & Background Knowledge

DOMAIN 5
Comprehension

DOMAIN 1
Planning and Organizing Reading Instruction Based on On-going Assessment

Competency 1
Planning, Organizing, and Managing Reading Instruction
Factors Involved in planning standards-based reading instruction

- Planning instruction based on state and local content and performance standards in reading. (Reading/Language Arts Framework for California Public Schools, 2007 and The California Content Standards
- Knowing the components of a balanced, comprehensive reading program and the interrelationships among these components.
- Doing short and long-term planning in reading
- Developing reading lessons that reflect knowledge of the standards
- Understand the progressive, sequential skills of a balanced, comprehensive reading program.
- Using reflection and professional development resources and activities to plan effective reading instruction

Organizing and Managing Reading Instruction
In organizing and managing reading instruction the teacher should provide for **universal access** of all students to effective reading instruction. This should include English Learners, advanced students, and students with learning difficulties. Management organization should provide for Differentiated Instruction in all areas of reading to meet the needs of all students. A variety of grouping techniques, instructional strategies and interventions should be utilized.

- **Flexible Grouping:** Throughout the day, students have opportunities to work in different kinds of groups with varied purposes, formats, and materials. Purposes for groups may be skill development or shared interest; formats may be teacher or student led with varying numbers of participants; materials may be the same for all groups or differ according to levels and themes. Grouping should be flexible, with students moving in and out of groups as needs and interests change.

- **Individualized Reading Instruction:** Children move at their own pace through reading material they have chosen, or through teacher-prescribed material, at the same pace as other children placed in the same group for reading instruction. Children are encouraged to read independently and they receive individual assistance as needed.

- **Timely Interventions**: Intervention should be planned and implemented as soon as a student shows signs of difficulty, usually in kindergarten or first grade. The student's needs should be assessed by the teacher, and individual or small group instruction should be provided in those areas which are weak. The intervention program should be followed by on-going instruction based on periodic assessments.

- **Use of carefully selected instructional materials** to match the interests, needs, and reading level of each student.

- **A learning environment that promotes student reading:** Books should be available representing a variety of interests and reading levels. Students should be motivated to read by being exposed to interesting and meaningful reading material

- **Use of independent and instructional reading materials:** The teacher should organize and manage reading materials by use of a well-planned classroom library and by careful selection of student textbooks.

- **Resources and equipment within the school and in the larger educational community:** district resources, community libraries, etc.

- **Use of Technology Resources:** Utilize resources such as internet research, United Streaming Videos, games, Docucams, etc.

Universal Access to the Language Arts Curriculum
Differentiated Instruction
"The ultimate goal of language arts programs in California is to ensure access to high-quality curriculum and instruction for all students in order to meet or exceed the state's English-language arts content standards." (California Reading/Language Arts Framework, 2007). All students are working towards the same standards. However the curriculum and instruction need to be modified on a regular basis to meet the different needs of the students. Students requiring differentiated instruction fall into three categories:
- Students with reading difficulties or disabilities
- Students who are English learners
- Students who are advanced learners

Differentiated Instruction involves considerations to be given to pacing, complexity, grouping, and modifications for disabilities:

- **Pacing:** The teacher slows down or speeds up instruction. The instructional pace of the advanced learner can be sped up if the student has mastered the standards. Students can be moved on to meet the standards for the next grade level. For students having difficulty, the instructional pace can be slowed down to allow for reinforcement of the content and re-teaching if necessary.

- **Complexity:** Instructional materials need to be varied and geared to the instructional level of the student. Advanced students can be encouraged to explore related topics, read related literature, expand their knowledge through research or special projects, develop critical thinking skills using the different levels of Bloom's Taxonomy, and make connections across the curriculum at a higher grade level. For students having difficulty instruction should be organized, sequential, and focused on basic concepts and skills needed to master the standards. Instructional materials should match the interest, needs, and reading level of each student. Instruction can be reinforced through the use of reading specialists, instructional aides, parent volunteers, or peer tutoring.

- **Grouping:** Groupings should be flexible with students moving in and out of groups as needs and interests change. They can be homogenous or heterogeneous. Advanced students may be placed together in a group to work on special projects or explore advanced concepts on a topic. Students having difficulty with a particular skill may be placed together in a group to receive small group skill instruction, re-teaching, reinforcement or additional practice on the skill. Cooperative groups may be composed of students at various levels. Children work together to study a topic, talk about a particular piece of literature, or work on special projects related to the curriculum. These groups give student who are having difficulty a chance to interact and learn from the more advanced students. Cooperative grouping often provides opportunities for a child who is having difficulty in reading to use talents and abilities in other areas such as art or music. Careful consideration should be given to the placement of students into a group. Grouping can be a powerful aid to instruction if properly managed.

- **Modifications for Students with Disabilities:** Some students need instructional modifications or supplements to the regular instructional program to help them reach their full potential. Programs available to these students include speech and language therapy, programs for the visual and hearing impaired, physical therapy, inclusion, mainstreaming and gifted education classes.Tape Recorders, amplification devices, or Braille word processors can help to meet the physical challenges of these students. Assessment should be thorough for these students and should be administered by a specialist who can then work with the classroom teacher to find strategies and activities appropriate for the students' needs.

Instructional Program for English Learners

"The purpose of differentiated instruction in English is to move English learners as quickly as possible through stages of language proficiency and to enable them to achieve mastery of the English-language arts content standards." (California Language Arts Framework, 2007). The instructional program must provide for skill and concept development in both English literacy and the English language. Support for these students must include pre-teaching of lesson vocabulary and language structure, building of background knowledge, instruction in academic language, and time for reinforcement, practice, and re-teaching. After-school programs, specialist teachers, tutors and paraprofessionals are other means of support. Appropriate instructional materials designed to meet the needs of the English learners should be provided.

Suggested Strategies and Activities for English Learners

Use of SDAIE Techniques: (Specially Designed Academics In English)

SDAIE techniques are modified content instructional strategies used in multilingual classrooms. Students are given additional language and academic support in a content class designed for native English speakers. These Activities include active participation, social interaction, integrated oral and written language, real books and real tasks, and an emphasis on building background knowledge and vocabulary.

Elements of a SDAIE lesson include:

- **Scaffolding:** Building on the student's prior knowledge. Begin with familiar concepts and build to more complex concepts.

- **Visual Aids:** Using pictures, films, charts, posters, real objects (realia - manipulatives for visual demonstration), etc. to explain concepts

- **Word Organizers:** Brainstorming, mapping, and clustering are techniques which generate many ideas about a given subject or text. They will help to determine prior knowledge as well as develop vocabulary necessary for the lesson. When Brainstorming, a group lists as many ideas as possible exploring a range of ideas related to the subject. Mapping is an organized visual representation of ideas that are viewed graphically as a whole. In Clustering uses the same process as mapping - circling the subject in the center and letting ideas radiate. The purpose of Word Organizers is to discover a wide range of ideas. One idea builds on the previous, leading to fresh new ways of looking at the subject.

- **Charting, Graphic Organizers, Graphic Maps:** Organizing thoughts and ideas into visually explicit patterns. Charting is a group activity in which the themes of a work are drawn on a large piece of paper after the anticipatory lesson. The class is divided into collaborative groups. Groups create charts, using lines, words, color, or pictures to make sense of the ideas shared with the class. Graphic organizers and Graphic Maps are used in the same way. They can be used to facilitate pre-teaching of concepts, vocabulary development, concept development, and post teaching. Some examples of graphic organizers are:

- **Charts:** illustrate and organize information.

- **K-W-L:** a graphic organizer outlining "What we Know", "What we Want to Know", and "What we Learned"

- **Venn Diagram:** A graphic organizer used to compare the similarities and differences in two objects or ideas.

- **Semantic Maps:** develop prior knowledge and organize information

- **Vocabulary Builders:** Pre-Teaching of Necessary Vocabulary and Language Structure

Additional Strategies and Activities to help English Learners include:
- Use Primary Language. Children should feel comfortable in their environment. Bring students' home language and culture into the classroom

- Provide bilingual/native language materials for students

- Design cooperative groups to place English learners with fluent English speakers.

- Songs, poems, choral readings, and patterned text to practice structure of the English language

- Use multi-sensory teaching techniques to increase comprehension:

- Include both verbal and nonverbal activities in each lesson

- Provide oral and written instructions for each day's assignment

- Increase "doing" or hands-on activities for students that do not involve reading or writing

- Use as many different means as possible to get a concept across (e.g., slides, films, overheads, maps, charts, pictures, etc.)

- Increase the use of of demonstrations: Model skills for students during direct instruction and during shared and guided reading and writing activities.

• Encourage group projects so that peer modeling and instruction can be utilized. Provide opportunities for students to do projects which are culturally meaningful to them. Student sharing of these projects helps cross-cultural understanding as well as reinforces oral language development.

Other strategies and activities to aid in planning for differentiated instruction include:

• **Explicit Instruction:** Giving direct instruction for difficult skills such as new concepts, multiple-meaning words, idioms, expressions, etc.

• **Schema:** Refers to how people process, store and retrieve information while reading. Pre-reading activities help to build on prior knowledge of student. Go from what the student already knows to new learning. Use of visuals, realia (real objects), mapping, graphic organizers, and well-planned questioning techniques help the student to store the information.

• **Shared Reading and Writing Activities:** Whole group instruction involving teacher modeling and guided practice.

• **Carefully Planned Lessons:** Lessons include pre-teaching, teaching, guided practice, independent practice, assessment for understanding, and intervention and re-teaching.

• **Carefully Selected Instructional Materials:** Materials should meet the needs, interests and reading level of all students. The use of high-interest / low vocabulary books helps to reinforce reading skills to those having difficulties.

• **Modified Lessons:** Integrate reading, writing, listening, and speaking into the lesson. Speak slowly and enunciate clearly. Increase "wait" time. Give students time to think and process answers.

• **Simplify Your Questions and Answers:** Use simple vocabulary and simple terms in questions and in responses to the students. Provide opportunities to practice.

• **Make use of all the senses:** Plan activities to include visual, auditory, kinesthetic/tactile/, taste, and smell.

• **Partner Talk (Think-Pair-Share):** Students will exchange ideas more freely by sharing their thoughts in pairs. Partners encourage each other and extend each other's thinking. Pairs take notes as they listen to the overview lesson. The teacher then has students think aloud and restate the overview lesson with their partner. As students work together, they express thoughts about the content, connections to real life situations, and interpretations or judgments they are making. This allows maximum involvement of students. Many

English Learners who will not express themselves aloud to the whole class will feel comfortable sharing ideas with a partner. Pair a fluent bilingual student with a limited English speaker of the same language background.

- **Labels:** important classroom materials, areas and safety regulations with bilingual signs should be labeled. (desk, bookshelf, closet, trash can, door, chair, etc.)

- **Cooperative Grouping:** Children work together in heterogeneous group of four or five students. In working with English Learners these strategies will help to develop their English proficiency and improve their learning.

Terminology for Organizing and Managing Reading Instruction

Balanced Reading Program: A reading program which includes strong literature, language, and comprehension with a balance of oral and written skills, systematic, explicit instruction in phonics and decoding skills, on-going assessment, and an intervention program for "at-risk" students.

Differentiated Instruction: Instructional modifications or supplements to help all students reach their full potential.

Explicit Instruction: the instructional process of 1) Teacher models the skill or strategy, 2) teacher guides the student as they practice and apply the new skill, and 3) students work independently and give feedback to the teacher.

Flexible Grouping: Students move in and out of groups as needs and interests change

Guided Practice: A phase of instruction in which the teacher and students practice a strategy together after the teacher has taught and modeled the skill. The teacher gives feedback about students' attempts and gradually leads the students to independent practice.

Independent Practice: The application of newly taught skills after skills have been explicitly taught and practiced under teacher direction.

Individualized Instruction: Students move at their own pace through self-selected or teacher-assigned materials with guidance and assistance by the teacher as needed

Modeling: The teacher helps the student understand reading material by providing examples. These might include "think-alouds", dialogue and responses, giving direct instruction, and providing examples of applying higher-order thinking skills.

Small Group Instruction: Teacher provides guided instruction in small groups to reinforce skills and concepts as needed. Groups are usually 5 - 8 students.

State Content Standards: An outline of mastery standards of the language arts program for each grade level, included in the Reading/Language Arts Framework for California Public Schools

Systematic Instruction: Planning instructing in a logical, sequential, and systematic format based on students' prior knowledge and progressing to a more complex context.

Whole Group Instruction: Direct, explicit instruction is provided for the class including modeling, building background knowledge, vocabulary development, guided practice, checking for understanding and re-teaching as needed.

Competency 2
Conducting On-going Assessment of Reading Development

Ongoing assessment of reading development refers to the use of multiple measures and the ongoing analysis of individual, small-group, and class progress in order to plan effective instruction and, when necessary, classroom interventions. All instruction should be based on information acquired through valid assessment procedures. Teachers must be able to use and interpret a variety of informal and formal assessment tools and communicate assessment data effectively to students, parents and others, i.e. school psychologist, speech therapist, Resource specialist, administrator, etc. (Source: *Supplement to the Program Certification Handbook for Elementary Reading Instruction*, 1998).

As children progress in their abilities in reading and language arts, a variety of assessment should be used, both formal and informal. These should include informal reading inventories, scoring rubrics, unit tests, portfolio assessments and norm-referenced assessments. Assessments should be based on state standards and should contain benchmarks at each level of progress. These assessments should provide the basis for instruction. Assessment drives instruction. Different types of assessment used before, during, and after instruction provide information that will help determine what to teach, what the students are learning and if the students have mastered the skills necessary to become competent readers.

Principles of Assessment

The *Reading/Language Arts Framework for California Public Schools*, Chapter 2, states that "assessment anchored to important learning objectives should provide the basis for instruction." Different types of assessment used at strategic points (i.e., before, during, and after instruction) provide critical information to determine what to teach, whether and how much students are learning, and whether the students have achieved mastery.

In the California Reading/Language Arts Framework three types of assessment are identified that should be used to plan instruction:
- Entry-Level Assessment for instructional planning (how to determine the level of students on meaningful indicators of reading and language arts skills. This should be assessed prior to instruction.)

- Monitoring student progress toward the instructional objective (how to determine whether students are making adequate progress on skills and concepts taught directly.) This would include periodic assessments developed by the publisher, teacher, or district at the end of each set of lessons. As the teacher plans and instructs students it is necessary to monitor their progress on an on-going basis to determine if adequate progress is being made.

Instruction should be modified on an on-going basis as a result of these assessments.

- Summative assessment toward meeting mastery of grade level standard (how to determine the effectiveness of instruction and students' level of achievement.) Summative assessments would include quarterly, midyear, and end-of-the-year tests developed by the publisher or the school district.

When using entry-level assessments, on-going assessments or summative assessments, the purpose is to drive instruction. These are the assessments a teacher uses to plan instruction, adjust instruction and re-teach if appropriate.

Standardized, or norm-referenced, tests are administered at the end of the year and are developed by companies contracted by the State Education or National Education Departments. The purpose of a norm-referenced test is to compare a group of students with a large population of students in the same group across the state or the nation, or any other specified sample population. For example, these assessments indicate how a group of fourth graders at a particular school or district compare to fourth graders across the state or the nation.

In kindergarten, first, and second grades, assessments should be individual rather than group standardized achievement tests. The assessments should be curriculum-based and include teacher observation and teacher judgment. More formal assessments of word recognition and reading comprehension may be used also as the child progresses. The purpose of the assessments in these grades should be to provide accurate information about the child's reading progress, rather than to make comparisons. Every kindergarten student should be assessed with a quick, informal assessment such as a screening assessment or check-list of skills to be mastered. The following skills should be assessed in Kindergarten, First and Second grades:
- **Concepts of Print:** Directionality, one-on-one correspondence, letters, words, punctuation, etc.

- **Phoneme Awareness:** Detecting rhymes, counting syllables, matching initial sounds, counting phonemes.

- **Phoneme Deletion:** Initial sounds, final sounds, first sound of a consonant blend.

- **Phoneme Segmentation:** Yopp-Singer Assessment - segmenting sounds, counting phonemes.

- **Letter Recognition:** names and shapes of letters

- **Letter-sound Correspondence:** initial and final consonant sounds

It is important to remember that phonemes refer to the sounds the students hear and not the relationship of the sound to a printed symbol

In first, second, and third grades, assessments should involve a systematic process of determining early reading progress. This should include:
- **Phonics:** reading nonsense words, decoding, spelling

- **Oral Reading:** fluency, correct words per minute on grade-level text

- **Reading Comprehension:** main idea, point of view, analysis, making inferences. Publishers end-of-unit test can be used for this assessment

- **Vocabulary:** antonyms, synonyms, multiple meanings

- **Spelling:** word patterns, single and multi-syllabic words, structure of words, regular/irregular words

In grades 4-8 assessment focuses on evaluating prior knowledge of the students for the planned content. Assessments should include:
- **Oral Reading Fluency:** words correct per minute on grade-level text.

- **Reading Comprehension:** main idea, point of view, inference, analysis, critique/criticism.

- **Vocabulary:** multiple meaning, word origins, context meanings, metaphors, similes, analogies.

- **Spelling:** spelling generalizations and patterns, multi-syllabic words, derivations.

- **Conventions:** capitalization, punctuation, sentence structure, grammar, penmanship.

In grades K-3, Entry-Level assessments will help the teacher to determine the level of instruction and the specific skills to be included in the lessons. In grades 4-8, these assessments help the teacher to determine prior knowledge of the students and the instructional support that is needed. Monitoring assessments should be based on content standards, and should aide the teacher in planning instruction, based on who has mastered the skills.

Assessing Reading Levels

To determine students' independent, instructional, and frustration level in Grades 1-8, an Informal Reading Inventory (such as the Johns Basic Reading Inventory or the Burns and Roe Infor-

mal Reading Inventory) may be used. This inventory includes three parts:
- sight word vocabulary assessment
- oral reading fluency assessment
- comprehension assessment

Results of an Informal Reading Inventory (IRI) should identify the student's
- Independent Reading Level (level the child can read "on his or her own"),
- Instructional Level (level the child can read with teacher guidance), and
- Frustration Level (Level which is too advanced for the child).

Independent Reading Level: If a child correctly pronounces 99 percent of the sight vocabulary words and correctly responds to at least 90 percent of the questions, the material is written at the child's independent reading level.

Instructional Level: If the child correctly pronounces 95 percent of the sight vocabulary words and correctly responds to at least 75 percent of the questions, the material is written at the child's instructional level.

Frustration Level: If a student needs help on more than one word out of ten or responds correctly to fewer than 50 percent of the questions, the material is too advanced and is at the child's frustration level.

A variety of other assessments may be used to determine the students reading skills.
- **Running Records** help the teacher determine how well a student is reading. As the child is reading aloud, the teacher puts a check above every word that the child reads correctly. When a child makes a miscue (error), the teacher uses a coding system to mark the type of miscue. The teacher then analyzes the miscues to determine how well the student makes use of various reading strategies, how well they construct meaning from text, and how well they monitor their own reading (e.g., self-correct if something doesn't

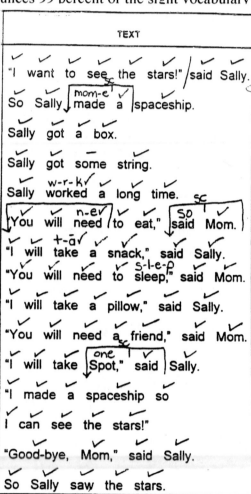

Figure 1.1: Running Records help a teacher determine how well a child is reading

make sense). The teacher can then plan the instructional program based on the student's strengths and weaknesses (FIgure 1.1).

• **Miscue Analysis** is similar in form and procedures to Running Records. Both the quality and quantity of miscues, or unexpected responses, are considered. Instead of considering only the number of errors, the teacher analyzes each error and what might have caused it. Miscue analysis helps the teacher gain insight into the reading process. Analysis of the types of miscues for each student, helps the teacher interpret why students are having difficulties. The reading is analyzed for mispronunciation, substitutions, self-corrections, syntactic patterns, and graphic cues.

• **Re-Telling** occurs when a student retells a story or a selected passage that he has heard or read. At first the teacher encourages the student to retell without offering assistance, but when the student appears to have finished, the teacher may help by asking open-ended questions to stimulate further retelling. Through retelling the teacher can learn much about a student's understanding and appreciation of the reading passage.

• **Cloze Procedure** helps the teacher to know if a text is easy or difficult for the student to read. By filling in words that have been deleted from a reading selection, the student demonstrates his ability to read the selection with understanding. The results of this procedure give information about the student's independent, instructional, and frustration levels for both narrative and expository text.

Other forms of on-going informal assessments may include:

     • **Teacher Observation:** Observant

Figure 1.2: A portfolio is a collection of a student's work over a period of time, usually kept in an expandable file folder.

teachers listen attentively and perceptively, during the course of each day. They evaluate as they listen and modify instruction, clarify explanations, give individual help, and provide reinforcement as needed. Note-taking and record-keeping is an essential part of observation.

- **Portfolios:** A portfolio is a collection of a student's work over a period of time, usually kept in an expandable file folder. It allows the teacher and student to analyze and reflect on the student's work and evaluate his progress. Contents of the portfolio should be dated. It should contain continuous, multidimensional samples of the student's work and should be aligned with curriculum and instruction (Figure 1.2).

- **Anecdotal Records:** These are written accounts of specific incidents in the classroom. The teacher records the incident, the time and place, and the possible implications. Teachers who keep anecdotal records become more sensitive to their students' interests and needs and are able to adjust their instruction if necessary.

- **Rubrics:** A rubric provides specific criteria for describing student performance at different levels of proficiency in different content areas. Students receive a number of points that represent minimal to high-quality work, depending on the type of response. A rubric helps students know in advance what is expected of them and helps teachers grade the students' work fairly. Rubrics should have 3, 4, or 5 point scales, with the highest number representing the most desirable level.

- **Conferences and Interviews:** Through conferences and interviews, teachers can find out about students' attitudes, interests, and progress in reading. Teachers gain insight into how children make interpretations and construct meaning. As the child explains his answers, teachers gain insight into the reasoning behind the student's performance.

- **Criterion-Referenced Tests**: These are informal tests of specific skills or content and are designed to give scores in terms of specific performance standards. These tests can be commercially prepared or teacher-constructed, and are intended to be used as guides for

  developing instructional prescriptions.

Using and Communicating Assessment Results

Assessment is essential to ensure that all students are provided with instruction designed to help them progress at an appropriate pace. Assessments should be on-going and may range from teacher observation and anecdotal records to more formal summative assessments. Results of assessments should be shared with all who are involved in the students' education. To effectively use and communicate assessment results the teacher should:

- Determine if the student is performing below, at, or above expected levels based on content standards

- Recognize when a student needs additional help in one or more areas of reading

- Plan and implement timely interventions to address identified needs

- Recognize when a student may need additional help beyond the classroom.

- Communicate assessment results and reading progress to students, parents, and support personnel, i.e. Resource Specialist, Speech Therapist, School Psychologist, nurse, administrator

Terminology for Conducting On-going Assessment of Reading Development

Anecdotal Record: a written account of specific incidents or behaviors

Authentic Assessment: a measurement of performance on activities that reflect real-world experiences

Checklist: an assessment form on which to record observations about specific skills development or behaviors

Cloze Procedure: a method for assessing reading comprehension by omitting selected words from a reading passage (usually every 5th or 6th word) and observing how many correct words the reader can supply.

Criterion-Referenced Test: a test to measure correct responses in terms of specific performance standards

Explicit Instruction: Instruction should include teacher modeling, guided practice, and independent practice.

Formal (Standardized) Test: a test, based on norms, for which reliability and validity can be verified

Formative Evaluation: gathering data during the time a program is being developed to guide the developmental process.

Holistic Assessment: Assesses a students ability to integrate separate skills into an entire selection. (for example; written expression, spelling and writing mechanics assessed as a whole)

Informal Assessment: Non-standardized, on-going assessment, usually teacher observation, portfolios, anecdotal records, conferences, etc.

Informal Reading Inventory (IRI): An informal entry-level assessment designed to help the teacher determine a child's frustration, instructional, and independent level of reading. An IRI includes 1) a sight word assessment, 2) an oral reading inventory, and (3 a comprehension assessment.

Kid-Watching: direct or informal observation of a child in classroom situations

Levels of Reading

    Frustration Level: a level of reading difficulty with which a student is unable to cope

    Instructional Level: a level of reading at which a student, with the teacher's help, can read with understanding

    Independent Level: a level of reading difficulty at which a student can read and understand without assistance

Miscue: an error in oral reading

Miscue Analysis / Reading Miscue Inventory: an informal assessment that considers both the quality and quantity of miscues made by the reader

Norm-Referenced Test: a test designed to report results in terms of the average results of a sample population

Performance Assessment: Demonstrates the student's competence in terms of an assigned response or product

Portfolio: a folder containing a collection of a child's work over a period of time

Portfolio Assessment: using contents of a portfolio to assess a child's progress over a period of time in terms of a standard, rubric, or benchmark

Retelling: re-counting, orally, the important aspects of the reading selection. Helps to develop comprehension and oral language skills

Rubric: a set of criteria used to evaluate a student's progress in a particular subject area

Running Record: a method of recording a student's miscues during oral reading assessment

Test Your Knowledge

1. Planning a language arts section in your daily classroom organization should include a variety of student groupings. Which would be the best to accommodate students with the same instructional reading needs?
    a) Small, flexible groupings based on student instructional needs
    b) Small groupings of students with each student at a different reading level
    c) Whole class instruction using one text
    d) Small groupings based on independent reading levels

2. A running record
    a) provides insights into a child's reading strengths and weaknesses
    b) gives grade-equivalent scores
    c) groups children by stanines
    d) determines the percentage of skill mastery

3. Which strategy would you want to make sure is part of your small/guided reading group plan?
    a) Change the students to different reading groups daily
    b) As an introduction to an instructional level book, prior knowledge is assessed regarding the story subject
    c) Include frustration level readings
    d) To meet once a week for reading

4. Systematic explicit instruction in phonics is:
    a) a series of lessons on selected skills, when appropriate
    b) daily instruction, based on students' needs
    c) based on teachable moments
    d) none of the above

5. Teachers can use "retellings" as a means of assessing students':
    a) reading motivation
    b) vocabulary and speaking skills
    c) reading fluency and accuracy
    d) retention and comprehension

6. One recommended strategy to encourage children to read voluntarily is:
    a) encouraging them to read to an adult daily
    b) supplying them with a list of classics
    c) holding a recreational reading period once a month
    d) setting aside time for them to read daily from freely selected materials

                                                              1) a 2) a 3) b 4) a 5) d 6) d

Notes on Domain 1

For sample questions on Domain I got to www.rica.nesinc.com

Notes on Domain 1

Notes on Domain 1

LEARNING TO READ
(Domain 2 and 3)

Pre-Reading (K-1)
• Phonemic Awareness
• Concepts of Print
• Letter Recognition

Reading (K-2)
• Phonics
• Fluency
• Word Identification
• Sight Words
• Reading Process

READING TO LEARN
(Domain 4 and 5)

• Comprehension
• Literary Response
• Content Area Reading
• Independent Reading

DOMAIN 2
Word Analysis

Competency 3
Understanding and Developing Students' Phonological and Phonemic Awareness Skills

Phonemic awareness is the understanding that "phonemes" are combined to form words and can be recombined to form other words. Phoneme awareness is different from phonics in that it does not involve written letters or words. Instruction in Phonemic Awareness means teaching awareness of words, syllables, and phonemes and includes rhyming, recognition, blending and matching of phonemes, segmentation, and substitution. (AB1086)

In the early stages of its development, phonemic awareness does not involve written letters or words and is, therefore, not synonymous with phonics. In later stages, however, work on phonemic awareness and phonics appears to be mutually reinforcing. (*Teaching Reading: A Balanced Approach*)

Research has identified phonemic awareness as the most potent predictor of success in learning to read. It is central in learning to read and spell. According to research, about twenty minutes a day, three to four times a week, will result in dramatic improvement for students who need further development in phonemic awareness.(*Building A Powerful Reading Program*)

Assessing Phonemic Awareness

In kindergarten, first, and second grades, the focus of assessment should be on individual diagnosis rather than on group standardized achievement tests. The teacher should collate class data and keep records on each child's specific areas. Data should be used to diagnose and plan instruction for children using flexible skill-level groupings as necessary.

Every kindergarten student needs to be screened for phonemic awareness with a quick and informal instrument.(Every Child a Reader) Some quick test instruments that reliably assess development of phonemic awareness in about five minutes include the Rosner, the Yopp-Singer tests, and the Roswell-Chall. (Building a Powerful Reading Program) Phonemic Awareness skills involve sound only. The printed symbol for the sound is not used. Skills that need to be included on an informal phonemic awareness assessment include:

- **Hearing words in speech:** Able to repeat a sentence one word at a time (I...see...a...cow)

- **Hearing Syllables in Words:** Able to clap syllables (di/no/saur)

- **Phonemic Isolation:** Able to isolate or match beginning, medial, and final sounds of a word (/m-a-t/: /m-a-n/; /c-a-t/: /f-a-t/)

- **Phoneme Blending:** Able to hear sounds and blend them into a word (/p/ /i/ /g/ - pig)

- **Phoneme Segmentation:** Able to hear a word and break it apart (pig - /p/ /i/ /g/)

- **Phoneme Substitution:** Able to change beginning and/or final sounds in a word to make new words. (ex. /m/ in mat to /s/ ; /d/ in mad to /n/)

- **Recognizing Rhymes:** Able to identify words that rhyme (hand - sand - land)

Role of Phonemic Awareness

Phonemic Awareness should be introduced in a sequential manner and should be related to the reading process. The progression of Phonemic Awareness Skills in Grades kindergarten - first, as outlined in the ***Reading/Language Framework for California***, 1997, should include:

- Recognize the number, sameness/difference, and order of isolated phonemes (How many sounds am I saying - /m-a-t/? Are they the same or different?)

- Track changes in simple words (/eat/ to /tea; /mat to tam/)

- Blend sounds orally to make words or syllables (/a/ /t/ =at)

- Identify and produce rhyming words (Does "fish" rhyme with "dish"?; What rhymes with "ball")

- Separate orally stated one-syllable words into beginning or ending sounds. (Which words begin the same - "mat, fish, mom"; which end the same - "fat, met, dish")

• Track words in a sentence and syllables in a word. (/I/ /am/ /six/; "/el/ /e/ /phant/)

• Count words in a sentence and syllables in a word. (How many words in "/I/ /am/ /six/"; How many syllables in "elephant"?)

• Recognize initial, medial, and final sounds in single-syllable words. (mat = /m/ /a/ /t/) Recognize long and short vowel sounds in orally stated single-syllable words (bit/bite)

• Produce a series of rhyming words including consonant blends (tack, stack, track) Add, delete, or change sounds to change words (cow to how; pan to man) Blend two to four phonemes into recognizable words (/c/a/t/ =cat)

• Segment single syllable words into sounds (cat = /c/a/t)

Developing Phonemic Awareness

Activities to develop Phonemic Awareness should provide active involvement for all students, should be fun and interesting, and should lead students to an awareness of the connection between phonemic awareness and reading. Appropriate activities include:

• **Use of Rhyming Books and Songs:** Children in K - 2 should be exposed to rhymes and songs with rhyming words on a daily basis. As the teacher reads, children should listen for the words that rhyme and make a signal, such as holding up a popsicle stick each time they hear the second half of a rhyming pair. The teacher says two words and the students show two markers of the same color if they rhyme or two markers of different colors if they do not rhyme.

• **Clapping Syllables:** A child claps the syllables of their name while the other students count. The teacher says any multi-syllable word and students clap and count syllables.

• **Singing:** Sing songs with repetitive phrases such as "The Farmer in the Dell." Have children clap syllables in the repetitive phrase instead of singing it.

• **Alliterative Language Play:** Read stories or sentences to the students such as "The jolly juggler juggles jugs and jacks." Students can also make up their own sentences using alliteration, such as "My mother likes meats, maps, marbles, and movies."

• **Segmenting Words Into Phonemes:** Have students say words slowly and pretend to stretch them like a rubber band. Let children take turns saying a word for others to "stretch" For example: Stretch "mat" into /m/, /a/, /t/.

• **Games:** Using a game board and picture cards, have children look at the picture and tell how many sounds are in the name of the object. They move forward on the game board for each correct answer.

- **Tapping Sounds**: Show objects to students and have them tap out the number of sounds with rhythm sticks.

- **Play "I Spy"**: Look at objects around the room. Say, "I spy an object with 3 sounds in its name." Have children guess what it is.

- **Blending Phonemes Into Words:** Say a single-syllable word. Have children "knock" on the table to show each sound, moving from left to right. Then have them go back to the first "knock" position and sweep their fists from left to right, saying the sounds and blending them together into the word. Have the students extend their fingers to count off phonemes, then use a sweeping left-to-right hand motion as they blend the sounds together. (For example: m/, /a/, /t/ into "mat")

- **Making new words by substituting phonemes:** Change mat to sat, sat to cat, cat to fat, fat to fan, fan to man, etc.

*For additional activities to develop phonemic awareness, see **Phonics They Use**, 5th ed., Patricia Cunningham*

Competency 4
Understanding and Developing Concepts About Print
Children must develop concepts about the way print works. Basic concepts of print include directionality (readers and writers move from left-to-right and from top-to-bottom); Spacing (used to separate words); recognition of letters and words; connections between spoken and written language; understanding the function of punctuation.

Assessing Concepts about Print
In kindergarten, first, and second grades, the focus of assessment should be on individual diagnosis rather than on group standardized achievement tests. The teacher should collate class data and keep records on each child's specific areas. Data should be used to diagnose and plan instruction for children using flexible skill-level groupings as necessary.

Every kindergarten student needs to be screened for concepts of print with a quick and informal instrument, usually a check list. Small "trade books" may be used in assessing concepts of print. The teacher should sit next to the child, with a small book, while the child demonstrates knowledge of the skills on the checklist. Skills assessed should include (Figure 2.1):
- **Directionality:** Left-to-right/Top-to-bottom/Return Sweep/Beginning of book/Ending of book.

- **Reading Concepts:** Print tells story/one-to-one correspondence of each word.

- **Book Concepts:** Cover of book/Title/Title Page

- **Words and Letters:** A letter/a word/first letter in a word/last letter in a word/key words in isolation.

- **Punctuation:** Period, Comma, Question Mark, Quotation Marks, Capitalization

Concepts of Print
The following activities will help children to develop concepts of print:
- **Count Letters in Words:** Show students words of various lengths and have them count as teacher points to each letter.

- **Sort Words by Length:** Show word cards to students with words of various length. Have students sort them according to the number of letters in the word.

- **Count Words in a Sentence:** During Shared Reading point to each word in a sentence as students count the words.

- **Make Sentences in Pocket Chart:** Give students a set of three or four word cards. Have

CONCEPTS OF PRINT CHECKLIST: CLASS PROFILE										
DATE:										
Directionality (demonstrated)										
Left-to-right page sequence										
Left-to-right in sentence										
Return Sweep										
Reading top to bottom										
Starting at beginning of book										
Finishing at end of book										
Reading Concepts (points to)										
Text (print tell the story)										
Each word (one-to-one correspondence)										
Book concepts (can identify)										
Cover of book										
Title										
Title Page										
Words/Letters (can identify)										
A letter										
A word										
The first word on a page										
The last word on a page										
A first letter										
A last letter										
A capital letter										
A small letter										
Names of some letters										
Key words in isolation										
Punctuation (can identify)										
Question mark (?)										
Period(.)										
Comma (,)										
Quotation marks (" ")										
Strategies used										
Relies on memory for reading										
Uses pictures to tell story in own words										
Uses pictures to help with words										
Uses language patterns										
Uses structure knowledge										
Uses beginning letter sounds										
Uses many letter sounds										
Uses background experience										

Figure 2.1 Marie Clay's Concepts of Print Checklist Assessment is a quick and informal instrument for checking a kindergarten student's knowledge of print concepts.

them put the words in order to make a sentence.

• **Shared and Guided Reading with Predictable, Repetitive Books:** During Shared or Guided Reading, point out left-to-right directionality, top-to-bottom, words in a sentence, beginning and ending of sentences, and likeness and differences in words. Look for words that are alike, words that begin the same, etc.

For additional Shared Reading activities see **Phonics They Use**, 5th ed., Patricia Cunningham

Letter Recognition

In order to appreciate that all words are made of sequences and patterns of letters, children must be able to discriminate the shape of one letter from another. Knowledge of letter names is an important means by which children recall or generate the sounds of letters when they begin to read and write independently. (**Teaching Reading**, Reading Program Advisory, Ca. St. Dept of Ed.) Children in Kindergarten should be able to recognize and name all uppercase and lower case letters of the alphabet. A checklist assessment for letter recognition will determine the child's knowledge of letter names and shapes in both upper and lower cases.

Instructional Strategies for teaching Letter Names and Shapes should include auditory, visual, and kinesthetic techniques and should provide interesting and stimulating activities.

- Learn songs using letters of the alphabet

- Use books about letters of the alphabet for Shared Reading such as **Frog Alphabet**, by Jerry Pallotta or **Chicka-Chicka-Boom-Boom**, by Bill Martin. Have the students say the names of the letters as you read the book.

- Trace letters in sand: Say the name of a letter and have students write the letter in sand or trace it on sandpaper for tactile reinforcement.

- Let children pretend they are letters: Give each student the name of a letter. When you show the students a letter, they stand up and say their letter name.

- Identify and write the letters in their name: Have students write their name and tell the names of the letters.

- Isolate and identify letters in words: Show students a word. Have them count the letters and then tell the name of each letter.

- Do activities with magnetic letters or letter blocks: Dictate letters and have students find them and put them in order according to how they were dictated.

For additional activities to develop letter recognition see **Phonics They Use**, 5th ed., Patricia Cunningham

Terminology for Phonemic Awareness and Concepts About Print

Directionality: Concept that reading and writing in the English language goes from left-to-right and top-to-bottom

Emergent Reading: Pre-reading stage where students learn the concepts necessary to become a successful reader

Letter-Sound Correspondence: Concept that each letter has a corresponding sound

Phoneme: Smallest unit of sound in speech (example:/b/ in big)

Phonemic Awareness: Understanding that speech is composed of a sequence of sounds and development of the ability to identify and manipulate these sounds. Not phonics.

Predictable, Repetitive Books: Books with controlled vocabulary which repeats words and phrase often and children can predict what the words will say.

Phonemic Segmentation: Breaking words down to their smallest parts. (example cat = /c/- /a/- /t/)

Phonemic Blending: Blending sounds together to make a word. (example /c/ /a/ /t/ = cat)

Rhyming Words: Words in which the "rime" (last part of the word) stays the same but the "on-set" (part of word before the vowel) is changed. (cat - mat - flat)

Sound Substitution: Changing individual letters to make new words. (cat - mat - mit - miss)

Guided Reading: Teacher assists and instructs as children read in small groups.

Shared Reading: Teacher reads as children watch and participate as a whole group.

Competency 5
Understanding and Developing Phonics and Sight Word Skills in Reading Instruction

Explicit Phonics Instruction

Explicit phonics instruction is an organized program where letter-sound correspondences for letters and letter clusters are directly taught; blended; practiced in words, word lists and word families as well as practiced in decodable text. The most effective instruction is explicit. It clarifies key points and principles to students. It is systematic in that there is a building from basic elements to more complex patterns...including beginning and final consonants, short and long vowel sounds, consonant blends, consonant digraphs, diphthongs, vowel clusters, silent consonant clusters (kn, wr, gn, etc.), r-controlled vowels, and ending clusters (ng, nk, ck, tch, etc.).

Research indicates that a direct and organized way of acquainting children with the major components of our alphabetic system is more effective than an indirect approach. (*Building a Powerful Reading Program*)

It is important for the children to practice the phonics they have learned. It is therefore essential that the initial books that children attempt to read on their own be composed of decodable text. (Teaching Reading)

Phonics Assesment

A Basic Phonics Inventory check-list should include:
    Consonant Sounds - Beginning and Final
    Consonant Digraphs
    Consonant Blends
    Short and Long Vowel Sounds
    Diphthongs
    Vowel Clusters
    R-Controlled vowels
    Silent Letter Clusters
See Appendix for Phonological Vocabulary Review

Instructional Strategies for Developing Phonics Skills

Instructional strategies for developing phonics skills should be taught in sequence, including phonemes, onsets and rimes, letter sounds, letter combinations, syllables, and morphemes. Activities may include:

- Letter Substitution: Making new words by changing beginning and final letters

- Making word families by using onsets and common rimes

- Games and activities using words with blends and digraphs

- Building Word Walls using phonics generalizations

- Changing beginning, middle, and end of words

- Using decodable text in Shared and Guided reading activities

For additional activities to develop phonics skills see **Phonics They Use**, *5th ed., Patricia Cunningham*

Word Identification Strategies

Word Identification skills involve the use of graphophonic cues, syllable division, morphology (affixes & roots), and use of context cues to identify unknown words. In the early alphabetic stage, children can guess on the basis of initial consonants. In later alphabetic reading, they can read through the whole word sound-by-sound. As their reading skills progress they learn to recognize word parts such as prefixes, suffixes, and roots as well as finding word parts in contractions and compound words.

As words become longer, children learn to decode unfamiliar words by syllable division. Generally accepted rules of syllabication include the following patterns:

- **VC-CV:** When you find two consonants between two vowels, they should be divided between the two consonants. (example: sudden/sud-den, admit/ad-mit)

- **V-CV:** When you find one consonant between two vowels, you usually divide them after the first vowel. (example: maple/ma-ple)

- **VC-V:** If the V-CV division does not make a word, put the division after the second vowel, creating a closed syllable. (example: camel/cam-el)

- **VC-CCV:** When more than two consonants are together, keep the blends together. (example: monster/mon-ster)

- **VCC-CV:** If a blend is in the first syllable, the third consonant goes with the second syllable. (example: pumpkin/pump-kin

- **V-V:** If two vowels are together and are not diphthongs, divide between the vowels. (example: lion/li-on)

Most Informal Reading Inventories include Word Identification Assessments. When administering a Word Identification Assessment the child should be able to recognize the word instantly.

Strategies for Instruction in Word Identification:

- Word Walls or Word Charts: These can include student-generated words which students and teachers can add to on an on-going basis, basic sight vocabulary words, or commercial charts.

- Labeling objects around the room which the children see every day

- Word clustering to support a "theme"

- Words around the room, such as color words, number words, children's names, days of the week, etc.

- Recognizing word families in which the onset changes but the rime stays the same...example: cat, fat, hat, mat, etc. Playing games which involve children actively and give children practice in recognizing and reading words. Word Sorts - have children put words which contain similar features into groups or categories....ex. Words that begin alike, words with certain letter patterns, animal words, food words, etc.

- Use of "predictable" books

- Picture dictionaries

- Learning phonics generalizations: vowel digraphs, r-controlled vowels, and irregular vowel patterns

- Learning syllable generalizations: vowel-consonant patterns, i.e. VCV, VCCV, etc.)

- Developing awareness of structural analysis: prefixes, suffixes, root words, compound words, contractions, syllabication

Sight Words

Not all words are decodable. Short words of extremely high frequency, such as the, of, are, and you, should be learned at the beginning reading stages. Because so many of them are irregularly spelled, they should be recognized at a glance so that the child's attention is not diverted from decoding. These words should be learned in kindergarten and early first grade. They may be words used frequently in reading or words that appear in grade level reading texts. Children must be able to identify sight words in order to develop automaticity in their reading. They are not necessarily decodable words - or words which follow the "phonics rules".

A good assessment for Sight Word Vocabulary is the ***Dolch Word List*** of 220 of the most frequently used words in children's books. It has been used since 1937, and is still one of the best and most widely-accepted lists of the most frequently used words in children's reading books. Another good sight word list is ***Fry's 300 Instant Words***.

The Reading Process

Good readers integrate three cueing systems while reading. These systems are Semantic, Graphophonic, and Syntactic.

- *Semantic*, or meaning, is by far the most powerful cueing system. This asks, "Does it make sense?" For instance in the sentence "When I play baseball, I hit the ball with a b_t." this helps to predict that the last word is "bat", since that is what one uses to hit the ball in baseball.

- *Graphophonic*, refers to letter-sound correspondences or spelling patterns. This asks, "Does it look right?" In the above sentence, the initial and final consonant help to confirm that the word is "bat".

- *Syntactic* cues relate to the grammar and structure of our language. This cue asks "Does it sound right?" "Is the structure right?"

A Balanced Reading Program

A balanced reading program in the primary grades should include the following:
- Consistent, on-going diagnosis and assessment

- A strong literature, language, and comprehension program including a balance of oral and written language.

- A systematic, explicit skills program including phonemic awareness, phonics, decoding skills, and vocabulary development

- A strong intervention program for "at-risk" students.

This can be accomplished through:
- A consistent, on-going monitoring system which includes both formal and informal assessments

- Shared Reading with Big Books

- Guided Reading with small group instruction

- Read-Aloud with a variety of quality literature

- Independent Reading

- Instructional Management System with charts and records

- Explicit Skills instruction

- Oral and written language activities to connect reading with oral and written language.

Terminology for Phonics and Sight Words

Affix: A morpheme that changes either the meaning or the function of a root word.

Alphabetic Principle: The concept that each speech sound or phoneme of a language has its own distinctive graphic representation.

Automaticity: the ability to recognize a word, or series of words, in text effortlessly and rapidly.

Consonant Blend: Two consonants that blend together before or after a vowel. (example: bl, fr, st)

Consonant Digraph: Two consonants that make one sound. (example: sh, ch, ph)

Decoding: Strategies used to recognize and read an unfamiliar word

Decodable Texts: Reading materials that provide practice in and reinforcement of specific decoding strategies.

Environmental Print: Print found in the environment such as on billboards, street signs, labels, etc.

High Frequency Words: Words which appear frequently in reading text

Irregular Sight Words: Words which do not necessarily follow the generally accepted rules of phonics and should be recognized automatically on sight and read without hesitation.

Morpheme: Smallest meaningful unit of language - can be a root word or an affix.

Morphology: Study of the structure of words

Onset/Rime: Onset: sounds before the vowel; Rime: remainder of syllable. (example: c-at)

Phonics: Systematic relationship existing between sounds and symbols and the application in decoding words.

Print-Rich Environment: an environment where a variety of printed materials are available, accessible, and used for everyday, authentic purposes. This might include color names, number names, labels, etc.

Reading Process: Process where various strategies are used to decode a text:

Graphophonic Cues: use of letter sounds (phonics) to decode unknown words

Semantic Cues: use of "meaning" to aid in the understanding of unknown words.

Syntactic Cues: use of language structure to aid in the understanding of unknown words

Root Word: basic word before affixes are added

Running Records: assessment tool for analyzing reading skills

Sight Words: words which are recognized instantly by the reader and read automatically on sight.

Structural Analysis: using syllables or morphemes to aid in the understanding of an unknown word.

Syllabication: dividing words into syllables

Vowel Generalizations: generally accepted rules for dividing words into syllables

Word Analysis: the process used to decode words. Word analysis skills include explicit instruction in phonics, syllabication, and word structure (prefixes, suffixes, compound words and root words).

Competency 6
Recognizing the Role of Phonics and Sight Word Skills in Spelling

AND

Content Area 7
Recognizing the Role of Syllabic and Structural Analysis and Orthographic Knowledge in Spelling

The Department of Education and the Reading Program Advisory of the state of California, support the following premises:

"Research demonstrates that combining ample early support of temporary spelling with systematic, formal spelling instruction results in more rapid growth in both correct spelling and word recognition than does either approach alone." (*Teaching Reading*)

"Students who have ample experience with invented spelling improve in both reading fluency and spelling. Direct instruction in word analysis and consonant blending is a necessary adjunct to children's spelling development." (*Building a Powerful Reading Program*)

"Recent research has shown that children progress faster in both spelling and reading if they are taught how to analyze sounds in words and taught how to spell them by using sound/symbol correspondence...the process of copying new words strengthens students' memory for those words and does so rather enduringly." (*Building a Powerful Reading Program*)

"Spelling Instruction means teaching a logical scope and sequence of word knowledge, orthographic patterns, and frequently used words connected to the phonics sequence used in reading and writing instruction." (AB1086)

Assessing Spelling
In Kindergarten and First Grade, spelling can be assessed by teacher observation. The teacher can observe the students' use of inventive spelling as the children learn to associate sounds with letters. Other indications include the ability to recognize classroom labels and environmental print. (words on signs or cereal boxes, for example.) As students advance in their spelling skills, Grades 2-6, formal or commercially prepared assessments can be used.

Teachers should be familiar with the stages of spelling development in order to analyze and interpret students' spelling development:
  • **Pre-phonetic:** Writing letters with no particular relationship of letters to sounds.

- **Semi-phonetic:** Writing words with some relationship of letters to sounds

- **Phonetic:** Writing words with relationship of letters to sounds with no knowledge of ir-regular sound symbol relationship

- **Transition:** "Creative Spelling" - Writing words informally with definite sound symbol relationship and some knowledge of irregularities

- **Conventional:** Learning to spell formally with knowledge of irregularities in sound-sym-bol relationship.

Systematic Spelling Instruction

In the pre-writing stages the student produces large scribbles or drawings with little or no place-ment or direction. At this stage instructional activities might include modeling left-to right directionality through shared writing activities and, as their skills develop, they begin to move in a horizontal direction across the page using dots, lines, and some letters. They then are able to spell using some letter-sound matching. As they progress, they begin to spell the most important features of a syllable and then begin to spell with beginning and ending consonants.

Direct, explicit and systematic Spelling instruction: Direct instruction should be systematic and follow a logical sequence from simple sounds to more complex spelling patterns. Activities to aide in the development of spelling in Grades K-1 might include:
- Modeling through shared writing activities

- Explicit instruction in letter-sound correspondence including modeling, guided practice and independent practice.

- "Sound" games and activities involving active participation of students

- Identifying likeness and differences in words

- Identifying spelling patterns and word families

- Use of word walls displaying frequently used words

In Grades 2-6 students begin formal spelling instruction in spelling using a systematic spell-ing program, supplemented with frequently used words and words from their reading materials across the curriculum. Instruction should include:
- Explicit instruction in the use of consonant blends, digraphs, regular short and long vowel patterns, and r-controlled vowels

• Explicit instruction in morphology - prefixes, suffixes, root words

• Explicit instruction in the spelling of words with irregular spelling patterns

• Study of word structure: syllabication, compound words, derivations, etc.

• Use of word walls identifying frequently used words

• Identifying spelling patterns and word families

• Use of Elkonin Boxes (sound boxes) to illustrate sound/letter correspondence and irregular spelling patterns. The teacher draws a series of boxes corresponding to the number of sounds in the words. The teacher and the student say the word as child points to each box. Then the student writes the letter of letters representing each sound. (Figure 2.2)

For more information on "Sound Boxes" see,
Phonics They Use, *5th ed., Patricia Cunningham*

Spelling Instruction in Context
Spelling should be taught in context through the use of the materials and texts in the classroom. Activities for teaching spelling in context in Kindergarten and First grades might include:
- A "morning message" - shared writing experience to develop concepts of print and phonemic-phonetic spelling

- Use of Big Books to teach letter and spelling patterns, sight words, and conventions of print

- Helping students identify common spelling words used in a thematic study

- Explicit instruction in phonics, using games and activities that involve active participation of each student

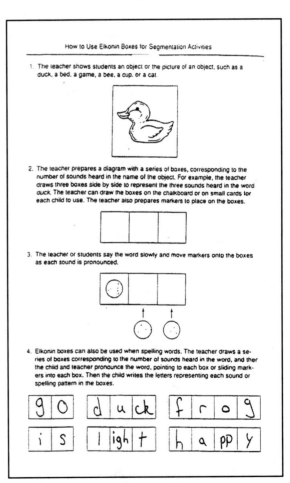

How to Use Elkonin Boxes for Segmentation Activities

1. The teacher shows students an object or the picture of an object, such as a duck, a bed, a game, a bee, a cup, or a cat.

2. The teacher prepares a diagram with a series of boxes, corresponding to the number of sounds heard in the name of the object. For example, the teacher draws three boxes side by side to represent the three sounds heard in the word duck. The teacher can draw the boxes on the chalkboard or on small cards for each child to use. The teacher also prepares markers to place on the boxes.

3. The teacher or students say the word slowly and move markers onto the boxes as each sound is pronounced.

4. Elkonin boxes can also be used when spelling words. The teacher draws a series of boxes corresponding to the number of sounds heard in the word, and then the child and teacher pronounce the word, pointing to each box or sliding markers into each box. Then the child writes the letters representing each sound or spelling pattern in the boxes.

Figure 2.2: Elkonin Boxes can be used for phonemic awareness activities as well as for spelling activities.

- Providing a print-rich environment with labels, color words, number words, children's names, etc.

- Writing words in sentences.

As children move into the more conventional spelling skills instructional strategies might include:
- Selecting spelling words based on words in students' reading and writing program - social studies texts, literature studies, etc.

- Use of "word walls" including words from thematic studies

- Creating signs, posters, book covers, etc. related to reading materials

For additional activities in spelling instruction see **Phonics They Use**, *5th ed., Patricia Cunningham*

Refer to the "Universal Access" section in Domain 1 to find strategies to provide for Differentiated Instruction to meet the needs of students with learning difficulties & disabilities, students who are English Language Learners, and advanced students.

Terminology for Phonics and Sight Words in Spelling

Encoding: Transferring oral language into written language. Students use their knowledge of sound-letter correspondence and phonics generalizations to spell a word.

Inventive Spelling: a temporary stage of spelling in which the emergent writer attempts to spell a word phonetically when the spelling is unknown.

Orthography: the study of correct spelling according to established usage.

Test Your Knowledge

1. The alphabetic principle is:
     a) phoneme recognition
     ib) ndividual letter matches an individual sound
     c) lower case letter recognition
     d) upper case letter recognition in order

2. Which type of reading instructional strategy would best meet the needs of a class introduction to the reading elements of concepts about print?
     a) Silent reading
     b) Independent reading
     c) Shared reading
     d) Guided reading

3. Knowledge of concepts about print in a beginning kindergartner is a strong indicator that:
     a) the child has been read to
     b) the child can read
     c) the child is gifted
     d) a & b

4. Shared reading is used to:
     a) model reading from left to right
     b) give individual reading practice
     c) master new sight vocabulary
     d) a & b

5. Concepts about print include all of the following except:
     a) being able to track words in a sentence from left to right
     b) recognizing word boundaries
     c) knowing how to spell simple words
     d) ecognizing upper- and lower-case letters

6. Why is it important to teach students high frequency words?
     a) These words are used so commonly
     b) These words are the only words that first graders should learn
     c) These words are phonetically regular
     d) All of the above

7. The most powerful predictor of later reading achievement is:
     a) a concept of print
     b) a knowledge of phonics

    c) phonemic awareness
    d) a knowledge of the alphabet

8. When children isolate sounds in a spoken word, they are practicing:
    a) segmentation
    b) rhyming
    c) sound blending
    d) substitution

9. Reading materials used for phonics programs have:
    a) predictable words
    b) decodable words
    c) high frequency words
    d) all of the above

10. Sight words are high frequency words that should be:
    a) recognized in one or two seconds
    b) defined in a sentence
    c) recognized in 20 seconds
    d) sounded out

1) b 2)c 3)a 4)a 5)c 6)a 7)c 8)a 9)d 10)a

Notes on Domain 2

For sample questions on Domain 2 got to www.rica.nesinc.com

Notes on Domain 2

Notes on Domain 2

DOMAIN 3
Developing Fluency

Competency 8
Role of Fluency in Reading Development and Factors That Affect Fluency

According to the National Reading Panel (2000), fluency is the ability to read text with speed, accuracy and proper expression. Effective reading requires automatic and fluent reading ability. Fluent readers recognize words automatically and read aloud effortlessly and with expression. The use of strategies and activities to develop fluency and automaticity is an essential part of a Reading program.

Oral reading fluency may be assessed by use of running records, informal assessments during instruction and group or independent reading. Students should be given frequent opportunities to read and reread decodable text and materials at their independent reading level.

Factors involved in fluency:
- **Reading Rate:** Children build their reading rate, fluency, and accuracy by reading and re-reading familiar text. Some strategies to develop this skill include reader's theatre, choral reading with a group, partner reading, one-on-one oral reading with a tutor or recording oral reading on a tape, reading along with a recording. Improving their reading rate helps children to better understand the content of the reading selection.

- **Word Recognition:** Developing basic sight word recognition helps students to increase their reading rate, fluency, and comprehension. Sight words should be recognized instantly, without decoding or analyzing the components of the word.

Fluency is composed of three parts. **Automaticity** is the ability to read words in text automatically. It involves fast, accurate and effortless word identification at the single word level. **Prosody** is the appropriate use of stress, intonation, and pauses in reading. Fluency involves not only automatic word identification but also appropriate prosody (rhythm, intonation, and phrasing) at the phrase, sentence, and text level. **Rate** is the speed at which a person reads. Good readers read fluently with adequate speed and with proper phrasing and intonation.

Competency 9
Promoting the Development of Fluency

Below are some activities to help to develop fluency:

- Provide students with proper modeling by reading aloud to them, providing a recording for them to listen to, or participating in cross-age reading (have good readers from an upper grade read to student in the lower grades)

- Use guided oral reading such as Choral Reading, Echo Reading (teacher reads a selection aloud and students chorally re-read the selection)

- Provide independent practice through reading aloud to an adult, reading along with a recording, 'whisper reading', or Reader's Theatre

- Participate in Choral Reading: Interpretive reading of a selection of text, usually poetry or songs, by a group of students

- Participate in Reader's Theatre: Bringing stories and characters alive through interpretive reading of a script. Unlike a play, there is no costuming, movement, stage sets, or memorized lines. The literature is communicated to the audience through facial expressions, voice, and gestures.

- Use Partner Reading: Students read text aloud with another student..

- Provide reading with a tutor: Student reads text with a parent volunteer, an aide, or an upper grade student

- Encourage at-home reading

To be a fluent reader, students must build their sight word vocabulary. Sight words are words that should be recognized instantly. This can be done with the use of flash cards, word walls, or word Bingo. There are a number of word lists for sight vocabulary including the Dolch Sight Word Vocabulary List which lists 220 of the most frequently used words in Children's books. The *Fry's 300 Instant Words* and *Fry's Instant Phrases and Short Sentences*. Most Publishers of Reading Texts have a Sight Word List incorporated into their Reading program. Sight words should be read in 1 or 2 seconds without having to pause to decode the word.

Differentiated Instruction

For students who need more intensive work in the area of fluency some suggested activities might be:

- Pair Reading

- Echo Reading with the teacher or another good reader

- Teaching sight word with orthographic patterns such as short vowel patterns, long vowel patterns, r-controlled vowel patterns, etc.

- Encouraging 'at home' reading

- Tracing, copying, and writing words in the air.

Advanced students can practice fluency by:

- Reading aloud to younger children

- Participating in Reader's Theatre

- Reading monologues associated with other areas of the curriculum such as history,

- Reading selections aloud from poetry or drama

For additional activities to develop fluency see **Phonics They Use**, *5th ed., Patricia Cunningham*

Terminology for Fluency

Automaticity: Fast, accurate and effortless word identification at the single word level

Choral Reading: Interpretive reading of a selection of text, usually poetry or songs, by a group of students

Echo Reading: teacher reads a phrase or sentence aloud and students read it back using proper rate, expression, and intonation as modeled by the teacher.

Fluency: clear, easy, and quick written or spoken expression of ideas. Freedom from word-identification problems that might hinder comprehension

Prosody: the appropriate use of stress, intonation, and pauses in reading at the phrase, sentence, and text level

Reader's Theatre: Bringing stories and characters alive through interpretive reading of a script.

Sight Words: frequently used words (usually abstract such as the, see, and, said, etc.) that should be recognized instantly, without decoding or analyzing the components of the word.

Word Recognition: Recognition and identification of the printed word

Test Your Knowledge

1. To improve reading fluency, students should read books at their:
   a) frustration reading level
   b) independent reading level
   c) instructional reading level
   d) none of the above

2. Susan is a word by word reader. To develop her fluency, you try the following:
   a) Echo reading
   b) rereading
   c) choral reading
   d) all of the above

3. Sight words are words which
   a) Follow phonics rules
   b) have a VCCV pattern
   c) are recognized instantly
   d) have a prefix and a suffix

1) b 2) d 3) c

Notes on Domain 3

For sample questions on Domain 3 got to www.rica.nesinc.com

Notes on Domain 3

Notes on Domain 3

DOMAIN 4
Vocabulary, Academic Language, and Background Knowledge

Competency 10
Understanding the Role of vocabulary, academic language and background knowledge in reading Development

AND

Competency 11
Promoting development of Vocabulary. Academic language and background knowledge

Role of Vocabulary Development
Vocabulary building is an important aspect of a language arts program. Teaching vocabulary involves more than having students find the meaning of a word in the dictionary and use it in a sentence. It involves understanding the words in context, building prior knowledge, and acquiring knowledge of English language structure. Vocabulary acquisition is directly related to reading ability and comprehension. A student can not understand text without knowing what the words mean. A student's knowledge of vocabulary is a strong predictor of how well the student will understand the content of the text.

Developing Vocabulary
Some activities to increase vocabulary knowledge might include:
- Classification Activities: Sorting words by theme or concept

- Clustering: A brainstorm technique centered around a topic or a concept related to material in the text. The topic or concept is written down in the center of a sheet of paper and students cluster words or phrases around it (Figure 4.2).

- Identifying Multiple-meaning words

- Learning Meaning From Context: Read a sentence or passage with an unfamiliar word and predict a meaning that makes sense with the context.

- Listening to and Reading a Variety of Texts

• Reading aloud Materials That Promote Vocabulary Development: Select and read aloud from literature rich in language. Have students pick out special words, such as descriptive words, "power" words, similes, metaphors, etc.

• Studying Related Words

•Semantic Mapping: Write a word or phrase representing a basic theme or concept and have students brainstorm words and phrases related to the theme or concept. Students see how words are related to one another (Figure 4.1).

• Thematic Word Wall: A Thematic word wall reinforces vocabulary words related to a theme or topic. The words are displayed on a chart that is posted in the classroom. Students or the teacher may add words to the chart each day as the topic is being studied.

•Using Reference Materials: thesaurus, dictionary, glossary, technology resources, etc. to explore related words and word meanings.

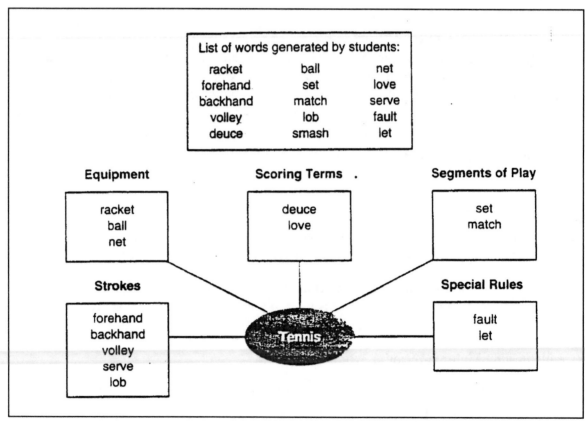

Figure 4.1: Semantic Mapping helps children see how worrds are related to one another

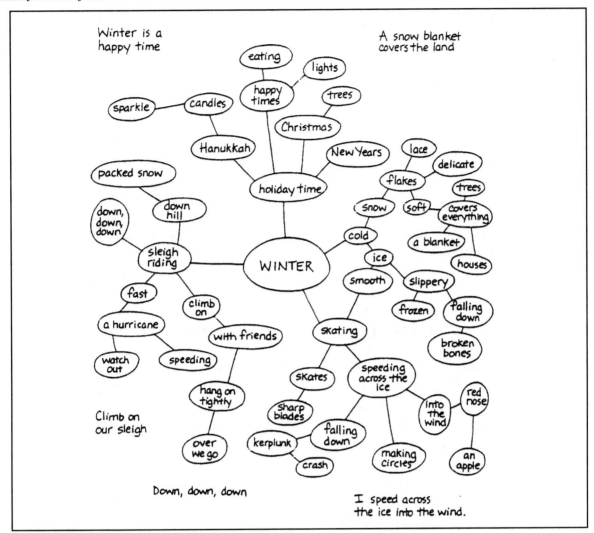

Figure 4.2: Clustering helps to build vocabulary knowledge

- Vocabulary Prediction: Have students write, in their own words, the definition of a vocabulary word. Students then check the meaning by referring to the reading

- Word Sorts: Words sorted by consonant or vowel sounds, onsets and rimes, categories, concepts or themes

- Word Banks: Collection of known sight words students use on a daily basis. Words can come from names, labels, rhymes, patterns, dictated stories or experience charts.

- Word Analysis (base words, prefixes, suffixes): Look for base words and discuss how affixes change the meaning of the word. Ex. Happy/unhappy

*For additional vocabulary-building activities see **Phonics They Use**, 5th ed., Patricia Cunningham*

Role of Academic Language

Academic Language refers to the language of literacy and books, tests, and formal writing. Proficiency in decoding and encoding skills is necessary but not sufficient for comprehending and writing about academic subject matter. Students also have to understand and use academic language. A number of studies have shown that academic language proficiency is related to achievement in reading as early as third grade. Vocabulary is a critical element of academic language. "Difficulties with comprehension were attributed to the challenging texts that use more difficult, abstract, specialized, and technical words; the concepts used in textbooks also become more abstract, and understanding them requires more sophisticated levels of background knowledge and cognitions" (Chall, Jacobs, and Baldwin 1990).

Developing Academic Vocabulary

Before giving students the reading selection, the teacher needs to identify words that may be unfamiliar to the student and discuss the meaning of the words. Daily "Vocabulary Building" activities greatly increase a student's comprehension in reading. Students should be involved in vocabulary development before, during, and after the reading of a selection. Academic vocabulary can be developed by direct teaching of vocabulary in specific content areas, using reference materials to study word meanings, teaching vocabulary through the use of context clues, structural analysis of words, and other daily vocabulary building activities.

Key components of developing academic vocabulary are reading, writing, and talking about books and school subject matter. Hearing language is not enough for students to learn academic language. They must use words rather than just receive them passively in order to retain new vocabulary. To help students develop academic language John Shefelbine suggests four strategies:

- Reading aloud to students: carefully selected books to emphasize academic vocabulary

- Have Instructional Discussions making use of academic vocabulary

- Have students read, both at school and at home

- Give opportunity for students to use academic language in their writing

(Information provided by John Shefelbine, California State University, Sacramento for the 2007 California Reading/Language Arts Framework.)

A range of approaches and activities must be used to develop students' facility in comprehending and using academic language. Oral language activities must be used to build knowledge of academic language and to familiarize students with grammatical structures they will encounter in written text. These activities might include:

• Use of literature selections to develop vocabulary

• Using language from literature not usually used in everyday language such as "gnashed their terrible teeth" (from *Where the Wild Things Are* by Maurice Sendak), "Her friends got tired and straggled behind (from *Maggie and the Pirate* by Ezra Jack Keats), or "Yonder is the farmer on a jet black horse" (from *Yonder* by Tony Johnston)

• Illustrating scenes and describing them to the teacher

• Creative dramatics

• Re-telling stories

Children will become familiar with different structures and conventions through their reading and writing experiences. For example, direct instruction of the lesson uses the book of literature to help students see how a compound word or contraction is used in the text. Reread the section of the book and have students find the example and identify it. Discuss how the particular example could be used in oral or in writing activities.

Role of Background Knowledge
Developing Background Knowledge and building on Prior Knowledge and Experience is essential when reading unfamiliar selections. Students should be able to relate the reading selections to their own background knowledge and experiences. Reading instruction should involve "into", "through", and "beyond" activities designed to build the child's vocabulary and provide background knowledge of the subject.

Developing Background Knowledge and Building on Prior Knowledge
Teachers can enhance comprehension by planning both direct and vicarious experiences related to the reading material. Students should be provided with activities that help them build concepts, discover interrelationships, and connect to their life experiences.

• Semantic Maps help students build concepts and discover relationships

• KWL Charts help students discover relationships between what they know and what they are learning

• A Prediction Charts helps children to confirm or reject their predictions as they read

• A Vocabulary Knowledge Chart helps students rate their knowledge of words in a chapter before reading

- Class discussions help students to build on their own knowledge and share from the background knowledge of other students

- Videos and other visual aids help students to acquire a knowledge base for the selection to be read

- Fieldtrips give students real life experiences that will aid in the study of a topic

- Guest Speakers can enrich the background knowledge of students by sharing their own knowledge and experiences.

- Videos from computer programs such as United Streming help to provide background knowledge and develop basic concepts.

Structure of the English Language

Explicit instruction in the structure of the English language helps students to build vocabulary. This refers to established rules for the use of the language. The structure of English builds students' knowledge of words and promotes reading fluency, listening and reading comprehension, and oral and written expression. The English language conventions and structures must be recognized by students when listening or reading, and applied by the students when speaking or writing. Teachers need a basic knowledge of English conventions and the structure of the English language (sentence structure, grammar, punctuation, capitalization, spelling, syntax and semantics and structural analy-

Prefix	Meaning	Meaning Chunk	Spelling/ Pronunciation Chunk
re	back	replacement	refrigerator
re	again	rearrange	reward
un	opposite	unfriendly	uncle
in (im, ir, il)	opposite	independent	incident
		impossible	imagine
		irresponsible	irritate
		illegal	illustrate
in (im)	in	invasion	instant
		impression	immense
dis	opposite	dishonest	distress
non	opposite	nonliving	—
en	in	encourage	entire
mis	bad, wrong	misunderstand	miscellaneous
pre	before	prehistoric	present
inter	between	international	interesting
de	opposite/take away	deodorize	delight
sub	under	submarine	subsist
fore	before/in front of	forehead	—
trans	across	transportation	—
super	really big	supermarkets	superintendent
semi	half	semifinal	seminar
mid	middle	midnight	midget
over	too much	overpower	—
under	below	underweight	understand
anti	against	antifreeze	—

Figure 4.3: Instruction in structural analysis of words helps to build vocabulary and improve comprehension

sis of words. Figure 4.3) Teachers must be able to provide instruction in these areas to improve students' vocabulary and literacy skills.

Informal assessments of students' oral language and vocabulary can be observed daily as the teacher listens attentively and perceptively during
- "Show and Tell"
- Classroom discussion (whole class and small groups)
- Conversations with the student
- Think-Pair-Share
- Cooperative Group Activities
- Literature Circles
- Reading Materials with good Grammar Conventions

The teacher listens for:
- Whole sentences vs short phrases or one or two word answers
- Correct grammar, syntax, semantics, topic
- Correct English pronunciation
- New vocabulary use vs "it", "um", "you know"...

Informal assessments of students' written language and vocabulary can be observed daily as the teacher reads or students read to the teacher at such times as
- Writing spelling sentences
- Writing in a daily journal
- Content subject writing
- Shared writing activities
- Guided writing activities
- Independent writing
- Creative writing
- Writing for portfolio collections

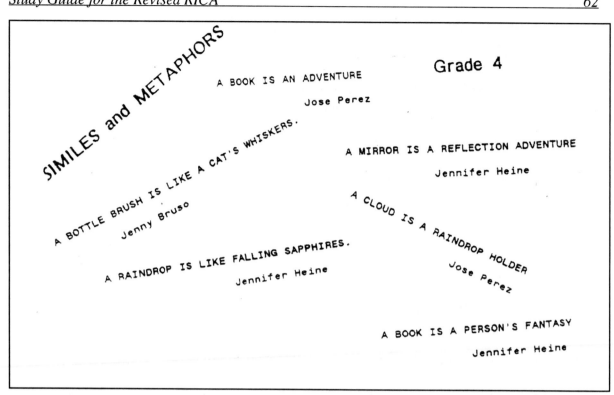

Figure 4.4: Using figurative language such as similes and metaphors helps to expand students' vocabulary.

Student Independent Reading / Encouraging Independent Reading

To expand vocabulary knowledge children of all ages should be encouraged to read independently. To promote independent reading a variety of activities can be utilized:

• The teacher can provide opportunities for independent silent reading during the school day by setting aside a time for Sustained Silent Reading (SSR) or DEAR (Drop Everything and Read). During this period students read material of their own selection, according to their interest. Children in grades K-3 read five to ten minutes or more and children in grades four to six read for 15 to 20 minutes or more. The teacher also should read silently during this time.

• Students can be encouraged to read by keeping a Reading Log of books they have read. Keeping a class chart and providing incentives for length of time read or pages read helps to motivate the child to read.

• Book Shares encourage children to read independently by sharing their books with the class and motivating others in the class to read the book.

• A Classroom Library, containing a large number of various types of multi-level reading materials, gives the students easy access to reading and motivates them to make good reading selections. The teacher should carefully select books and magazines for the library and should guide the students in choosing books to match their interests and reading level.

- Reading aloud to students exposes the class to high-quality texts and helps them in becoming aware of their own preferences of reading materials.

Supporting At-Home Reading

Encouraging the support of parents or guardians in "at-home" reading programs motivates students to extend their reading from school to home and aids in vocabulary building. Consistent and continuous communication with the home is essential to a good home reading program. In the primary grades home reading can include the parent or guardian reading to the child, as well as the child reading to them. Helping promote reading at home may include:

- Reading picture books to and with the child

- Pointing out and reading familiar signs such as "McDonald's", "Stop", "Exit", "Pepsi Cola", etc.)

- Sharing newspapers and magazines at an appropriate level and interest, and encouraging the child to find familiar words that appear in advertisements.

- Singing songs, nursery rhymes, chants.

- Playing "guessing" games

- Reading together cereal boxes, menus, place mats, street signs, coupons, and other forms of print

- Visiting the children's section of the library and letting the child get a library card and check out books to take home.

- Providing a quiet time and place at home each evening for the child to read. (Turn off the TV during this time)

Refer to the "Universal Access" section in Domain 1 to find strategies to provide for Differentiated Instruction to meet the needs of students with learning difficulties & disabilities, students who are English Language Learners, and advanced students.

Test Your Knowledge

1. Which of the following strategies would assess students' prior knowledge of a subject?
    a) Directed Reading Thinking Activity
    b) At the end of a story, ask the students what parts they didn't understand
    c) Reciprocal Teaching
    d) KWL Chart

2. "K-W-L" refers to:
    a) what we know, where we went, and how we listened
    b) what we know, what we want to write, and what we liked
    c) what we know, what we want to know, and what we learned
    d) what we know, what we watched, and what we listed

3. When is it most useful to determine the key concept and vocabulary?
    a) During lesson preparation and planning
    b) Before the students read the text
    c) As the students read the text
    d) After the students have read the text

4. One recommended strategy to encourage children to read voluntarily is:
    a) encouraging them to read to an adult daily
    b) supplying them with a list of classics
    c) holding a recreational reading period once a month
    d) setting aside time for them to read daily from freely selected materials

5. Context clues assist in vocabulary development because:
    a) students use surrounding information in the sentence and paragraph to predict the meaning of an unfamiliar word
    b) vocabulary development occurs during silent reading
    c) students use their knowledge of semantics to figure out the meaning of the word
    d) a student can make a list of the unknown words to find definitions in the dictionary later

1)d 2)c 3)a 4)d 5)a

Notes on Domain 4

For sample questions on Domain 4 got to www.rica.nesinc.com

Notes on Domain 4

Notes on Domain 4

INSTRUCTIONAL PROCESS

How do you move students from one stage to the next?

"I DO IT"
Teacher models the skill

"WE DO IT"

Guided practice

"YOU DO IT"

Independent practice

DOMAIN 5
Comprehension

Competency 12
Understanding Comprehension and Factors Affecting Reading Comprehension

Assessing Reading Comprehension
The following are ways in which a teacher may assess reading comprehension:

- **Informal Reading Inventory:** (IRI) Assesses a students sight-word vocabulary, oral reading fluency, and comprehension. This assessment helps to determine the students independent, instructional, and frustration level (see Domain 1 for further details)

- **Questioning at Varied Levels**
  - Literal: answers require simple response directly stated in the reading selection. ("right there" questions)
  - Main idea: answers require identifying a central theme in the reading selection
  - Making Inferences: answers require identifying information implied by the author. ("think-about-it" questions).
  - Analysis: answers require breaking down information into component parts and identifying their unique characteristics.
  - Critique: answers require students to compare the ideas in the reading selection with known standards and draw conclusions about their accuracy and appropriateness.
  - Point of view: answers require students to judge the value of material in the reading selection based on personal opinions.

- **Re-Tell:** Student reads or listens to a story and re-tells the story to the teacher. The teacher is able to analyze the students understanding and appreciation of the story.

- **Unit Tests:** Check the students' knowledge and understanding of a specific skill or content area. Unit tests may be teacher-constructed or included in a textbook program.

- **Literature Logs:** Students read a selection and record personal interpretations, strategies for constructing meaning, questions that arise and issues they may want to discuss with others.

- **Book Reports:** Students read a book and write a summary, focusing on the main idea, character development, plot, problem, and resolution.

Fluency and Other Factors Affecting Comprehension

Reading Rate and Fluency: Children improve their reading rate, fluency and accuracy by reading and re-reading familiar text. Improving reading rate and fluency helps children better understand the content of the reading selection.

Word Recognition: Developing basic sight-word recognition helps students increase their reading rate, fluency, and comprehension. These are words which should be recognized instantly, without decoding or analyzing the components of the word.

Prior Knowledge and Experience: Students should be able to relate the reading selection to their own schema, (background knowledge and experiences). Reading instruction should involve "into" activities designed to build the child's vocabulary and provide background knowledge of the subject.

Vocabulary Knowledge: Before giving students a reading selection, the teacher should identify words that may be unfamiliar and discusses the meaning of the words. Daily "Vocabulary Building" activities greatly increase a student's comprehension in reading.

The following are Different Levels of Comprehension
- **Literal:** Explicitly stated main idea, details, sequence, cause & effect

- **Inferential:** inferred main ideas, details, comparisons, cause/effect relationships; drawing conclusions, making generalizations, predicting outcomes

- **Evaluative:** Bias, unsupported inferences, propaganda, faulty reasoning, fact & opinion, character analysis, use of language.

Competency 13
Facilitating Reading Comprehension

Reading comprehension can be facilitated by the use of "Into-Through-Beyond" activities to build the students prior knowledge, increase their awareness of the reading material, and provide follow-up activities to reinforce what they have learned. Such activities include:

- **Developing background knowledge:** Teachers can enhance comprehension by planning both direct and vicarious experiences related to the reading material. Students are provided with activities that help them build concepts and discover interrelationships between what they know and what they are learning. Vocabulary instruction, semantic mapping , K-W-L charts, class discussions, videos, field trips, demonstrations, guest speakers, and computer research are examples of activities that will help to expand a student's knowledge and experience.

- **Encouraging Predictions:** As students become involved in their reading, they are encouraged to anticipate or predict what will happen next in their reading. These predictions should be confirmed or rejected as the reading is continued.

- **Questioning Using levels of Bloom's Taxonomy:** Questions presented to the students encourage them to think beyond the literal meaning of the text. Students should be taught the question-answer-feedback strategies, using the different levels of Bloom's Taxonomy - knowledge, comprehension, application, analysis, synthesis, and evaluation.

- **Conducting Discussions:** Discussions should be interactive between the teacher and the students, with the teacher guiding the discussion through the use of questions, probing for elaboration, and having students use the text to support their answers.

- **Inference Questions:** These questions help students develop the ability to "read between the lines" in a text. They ask for information that is implied but not directly stated. These are "think-about-it" questions.

- **Compare and Contrast Activities** are developed to encourage the student to find likeness and differences in two related topics. This can be facilitated through the use of charts or graphic organizers, such as a Venn Diagram or a Comparison Chart.

- **Developing Vocabulary:** Students should be involved in vocabulary development before, during, and after the reading of a selection. Vocabulary can be developed by direct teaching of vocabulary in specific content areas, using reference materials to study word meanings, teaching vocabulary through the use of context clues, structural analysis of words, and other daily vocabulary building activities

- **Identifying Main Idea**: Students should learn to identify the topic sentences in expository text. Creating their own titles for the text will help them to understand the concept of "main idea".

- **Identifying Fact and Opinion:** Students need to learn to discriminate between statements that can be verified (fact) and statements that can not be verified (opinion). Looking for words such as "believe", "think", "may", etc. can help students to develop this skill.

- **Summarizing:** After reading a given selection, students should be taught to summarize it in their own words, either orally or written

- **Into-Through-Beyond Activities:** The teacher prepares students for a reading selection by using pre-reading activities (into) such as sharing information on the topic, making predictions based on the title or the pictures, or generating questions about the story that they expect to answer from their reading. Reading of the selection (through) can be done through silent reading, group shared reading, or teacher reading. At strategic points the teacher pauses for whole class or small group discussions involving predictions, purpose questions, or personal reactions. The teacher designs questions to help the children relate the story to their own experiences and to lead them to think critically and creatively about the reading material. After the material has been read (beyond), the teacher provides activities that extend the children's understanding and help them elaborate on the ideas presented in the selection. These might include characterizations, re-telling, illustrations, narrative journals, drama presentations, etc.

Study Skills to Improve Reading Comprehension

- **Self-monitoring:** Students monitor their own reading behaviors and use appropriate strategies to decode and comprehend a text.

- **Re-reading:** Returning to a text and reading it again immediately, or after several days. This activity helps improve speed, accuracy, expression, comprehension, and linguistic growth.

- **Note-Taking:** Jotting down main ideas, key words and phrases and important facts pertaining to the material that is being read.

- **Rethinking:** After students make predictions about the text or material to be read, the teacher or students read the material and the teacher guides a discussion to confirm or reject the predictions. The students then re-think and revise their original predictions.

- **Summarizing:** After reading a selection, the students restate what the author has said in a more concise form, deleting trivial and redundant material. This skill can be developed by providing several summaries of the same passage, and letting the students determine which summary is best and why.

- **Mapping:** Using a graphic organizer or diagram to help students see relationships between words, ideas, and concepts in a reading selection.

- **Learning Logs:** Following the reading or discussion of a topic, students write summaries, comments, or questions related to the reading or class discussion. The teacher reads the comments and adjusts future lessons in response to the degree of understanding or lack of understanding reflected in the student logs.

- **Guided Practice of Comprehension Strategies:** The teacher helps students to construct meaning from a text by guiding them to focus on the relevant features of the text and to relate those features to their prior experiences

- **Independent Practice of Comprehension Strategies:** The teacher assigns the students a selection to read independently. Students read the entire selection by themselves. Structured support is provided by using a study guide that poses questions and gives activities which guide students through the reading of the text.

- **Providing Differentiated Instruction:** Facilitate reading comprehension for the full range of learners in the classroom. (see Domain 1 for more information on activities for Differentiated Instruction.)

Competency 14
Understanding How to Promote comprehension and Analysis of narrative/literary texts and the development of literary response skills.

Assessing Literary Response and Analysis
- Literature Circles: Students read a piece of literature and meet as a group to discuss it. The discussions are open-ended and focus on bringing the literature and the reader together. The group can respond to teacher prepared questions or can discuss reactions to the book - sharing favorite parts, raising questions about parts they did not understand or sharing their own reflections on the reading. The teacher monitors the literature circles as they discuss, and assesses the students' development, thinking processes and comprehension levels.

- Literature Logs: After reading a section or chapter in a book, students write their reactions to the story in a journal, or literature log. These are written by the individual student to help them think through what they are reading. The teacher can assess a student's developing writing skills and their comprehension of the story.

- Book Reports: A written or oral summary of a book that was read, focusing on the most important or interesting part of the text. The teacher assesses the student's written and oral language development, and their comprehension of the reading material. Book Reports can also involve "projects" such as a poster advertising the book, a "book cover" with a picture and summary, or a short dramatization of an interesting event in the book.

Responding to Literature
The following are some ways in which the teacher might ask students to respond to literature.

- **Identifying Main Problem:** Students build on their comprehension of a story by creating a "plot diagram" and identifying the main problems created in the plot of the story.

- **Character Analysis:** Through a discussion of the traits, emotions, and reactions of the story characters, students learn to identify and categorize various types of character traits and apply them to the characters of the story. This can be done by creating word webs of various traits and by using questioning techniques to help students see the connection between their own traits, those of people they know, and those of the characters in the story. Students analyze a character's emotions and emotional states as they react to the events of the story.

- **Compare/Contrast Types of Literature:** Using a Venn diagram or a comparison chart students identify the likeness and differences of various pieces of literature or of characters in the story.

Literary Analysis

The teacher guides the students to identify and recognize various elements of literary analysis through the selection of and analysis of appropriate literature. These elements should include:

- **Genre:** Literary forms such as Historical Fiction, Biographies, Autobiographies and Informational books. These can be studied as they relate to content areas.

- **Realistic Fiction and Multicultural Literature:** these serve as a model for helping children to understand others and solve problems in their own lives.

- **Poetry and Plays:** these encourage students to explore their emotions, and offer them the opportunity of acting out favorite stories. (see fig. 3.9)

- **Modern Fantasy and Folklore:** these allow students to escape into worlds of imaginary characters and events.

Understanding of these genres should be a part of the literature program. The teacher enhances the students' understanding of these genres by reading literature of all forms aloud and pointing out the characteristics of each genre.

- **First and Third Person Narrative:** Students recognize when a narrative text is written from the point of view of the writer and when it is written from the point of view of another person.

- **Figurative Language:** The teachers identifies the various types of figurative language by taking examples from literature the students are currently studying and expanding them into additional oral or written activities that will reinforce the concept. (fig. 3.10)

  - **Simile:** A comparison using "like" or "as"...ex. "As quiet as an eyelash"

  - **Metaphor:** Poetic definition of an object, using something entirely different but with the same attributes. ex. "A sneeze is an explosion in the nose"

  - **Personification:** giving the attributes of a person to an inanimate object or abstract idea - "A dandelion is a soldier with a golden helmet"

- **Fact and Fantasy in Historical Fiction:** In reading fiction books based on historical events, students determine the events that actually have historical validity and those which are the imagination of the author.

Activities for Developing Literary Response

- **Quick-Write:** A five to ten minute free-writing exercise to generate ideas and to discover what students already know. Students write about a given topic for a certain period of time. Their pens or pencils must move continuously.

• **Personal Connections:** Students recognize a connection or similarity between a personal experience and either a character's experience or some other aspect of a reading selection. Identify a theme or an aspect of literature being studied and have students do a quick-write that makes a connection between the theme or aspect and a personal experience. (first day of school, a happy, scary, or sad event in their life, a bad day, etc.)

• **Think-Aloud/Pair Share:** Students are placed into pairs to exchange thoughts about personal experiences, interpretations, judgments, or ideas related to an assigned reading selection.

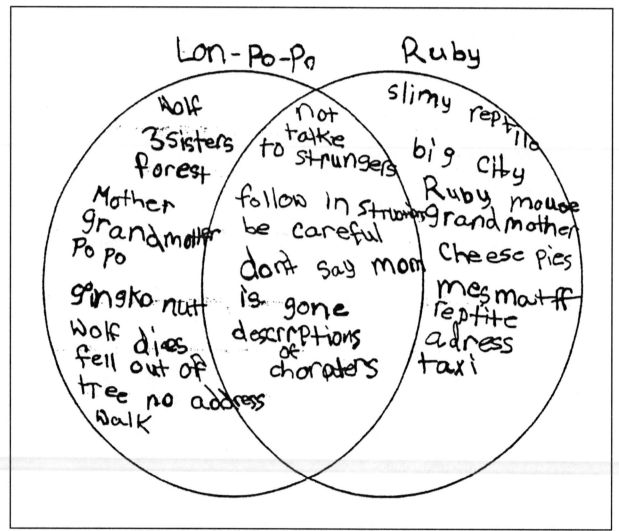

Figure 5.1: Venn diagrams develop comprehension skills by teaching students to compare various aspects of literature.

- **Dialectical Journal:** A two-column form on which the student, while reading a selection, makes notes in the left hand column on his own responses or reflections on parts of the reading that he finds interesting or meaningful. In the right-hand column the student tells why he found the selection interesting or meaningful.

- **Journals:** Students make notes, record observations, dialogues, reflections and lists about fictional stories, or other things that they have read.

- **Open Mind:** A diagram used for a visual character analysis. On a blank "open mind" diagram, students draw symbols or write words and phrases from the text that represent that character or what the character is thinking or feeling.

- **Hot Seat:** Individual students adopt the persona of a character in literature and answer questions from the character's perspective. The class is divided into groups of three to five students. Each student selects a character whose persona he or she will adopt. Then, in turn, each "character" responds to questions posed by other members of the group (about 2 min. per character).

- **Grand Conversation:** A meaningful discussion of literature. A group of student volunteers come to the front of the class and discuss a literary work or an aspect of it. One of them keeps a record of the topics and issues discussed. At the close of the conversation, the leader reviews the record and reports any patterns that emerge.

- **Venn Diagram:** A graphic organizer composed of two overlapping circles for charting similarities and differences between characters, stories, or other elements. Students may work individually, with partners, or with groups. Students label the diagram with the names of the two items or aspects to compare and contrast. They list the elements particular to each item in the outer parts of the circles. In the overlap of the circles they list the characteristics common to both items or aspects. (Figure 5.1)

Competency 15
Understanding How to Promote Comprehension of Expository/Informational Text Development of Study Skills and Research Skills.

Assessing Content-Area Literacy
Various types of assessment may be used in assessing content-area literacy. Assessments may include:
- Research Paper Rubric
- Unit or chapter tests from text
- Teacher-developed tests from content of the text
- Anecdotal records of individual classroom participation

Different Types of Texts and Purposes for Reading
Students should be exposed to many different types of texts and purposes for reading in content-area instruction. These may include:
- Magazines, newspapers, online materials
- Gain meaning from documents, i.e. warranties, contracts, product information, instructions
- Use of Websites

Study Skills
Students learn a variety of skills to gain proficiency in studying for content-area reading. Important to developing study skills are:
- **Skimming:** reading selectively to pick up main ideas and general impressions about the material

- **Scanning:** moving the eyes rapidly over the selection to locate a specific bit of information such as a name or a date.

- **Note-Taking:** Jotting down important facts as the material is being read. Post-its, marginalia or a Double-Entry Journal may be used.

- **Clustering:** A brainstorm technique centered around a topic or a concept related to material in the text. The topic or concept is written down in the center of a sheet of paper and students cluster words or phrases around it.

- **Pre-Viewing:** Looking through the selected reading material to determine the content of the text.

• **Researching Topics:** A thorough study of a topic or concept using reference materials, textbook information, note taking, prior knowledge, internet research and other sources of information.

• **Studying for Tests:** Using methods such as graphic organizers, clustering or mapping to study content for a test. Learning the meaning of test directions such as compare, contrast, describe, and explain.

• **Learning Test-Taking Strategies**

Teaching in the Content Area

In order to effectively teach in the content areas, one must understand the concept of "Into-Through-Beyond". This concept is essential to good instruction. A child's interest will be held and he will become actively involved in the lesson if he is prepared for the lesson by "lead-up" activities (into), and if he is involved in follow-up activities (beyond).

The "into" part of the lesson helps to give children background knowledge, build on their prior knowledge, develop necessary vocabulary knowledge, and focus them on the topic. Imagine trying to teach children from a tropical climate how to build a snowman if they have never seen snow. They would have no concept and a great deal of explanation, description, and vocabulary development would be necessary before you even begin your instruction. This is the purpose of the "into" part of the lesson.

The "through" part of a lesson is the actual instruction that takes place after the class has had some vocabulary building, background knowledge development and is focused on the learning. In our example of the snowman, this would involve actually teaching them how to build a snowman.

The "beyond" part of the lesson is a follow-up to the instruction. Again, in the case of the snowman, this would possibly be having the children build a snowman out of crushed ice or possibly paper-mache'.

Following are listed some "into", "through", and "beyond" activities which will aid in teaching in the content area:

Into Activities
• **Brainstorming:** Through clustering, mapping, or class discussion, students brainstorm what they know, collectively, about a topic

• **Chapter Walk:** Preview chapter noting headings, sub-headings and chapter questions. Look at pictures, captions, diagrams, charts, timelines, etc

- **DRTA (Direct Reading-Thinking Activity):** A technique to direct children's reading of literature selections or of content area selections.

  Step1: Write the title of the chapter on the chalkboard. Students make predictions as to what they think the chapter will be about.

  Step 2: Examine the pictures in the chapter and revise the predictions based on the new information.

  Step 3: Read the introduction to the chapter and check the accuracy of the predictions.

  Step 4: Discuss the accuracy of the predictions. Read parts of the introductory paragraphs which support the correct predictions..

- **KWL:** Before reading a selection, students list in the first and second column of a three-column chart what they already know about the topic and what they want to know about the topic. After reading, students list in the third column what they learned about the topic. (fig. 1.10)

- **QAR:** (Question-Answer Relationships): A questioning technique in which students explore the relationship of three levels of questioning: "Right There" questions in which the answers are found directly in the text, "Think and Search" questions in which students can infer answers from the written text; and "In My Head" questions which students develop from their own knowledge.

- **SQRRR:**
  - **Survey:** students scan the reading selection noting the chapter title and main headings, reading the introductory and summary paragraphs, and inspecting maps, graphs, or illustrations.
  - **Question:** students write a list of questions they expect to be answered in the reading.
  - **Read:** students read the selection, looking for answers to their questions and taking brief notes.
  - **Recite:** students try to answer their questions without looking back at the text.
  - **Review:** students re-read the selection to verify their answers and to reinforce the main points of the text.

- **Thematic Word Wall:** Reinforces vocabulary words related to a theme or topic. Words are displayed on a chart which is posted in the classroom. Students or teacher may add words to the chart each day, as the topic is being studied.

- **Think-Pair-Share:** Children think about what they know about a topic. They then divide into Pairs and tell their partner what they know. Then they Share what they know with the whole class. In the upper grades the students can write what they know in a "quick-write", then share with a partner, then share with the whole class.

- **Video:** View a video on the topic before reading text

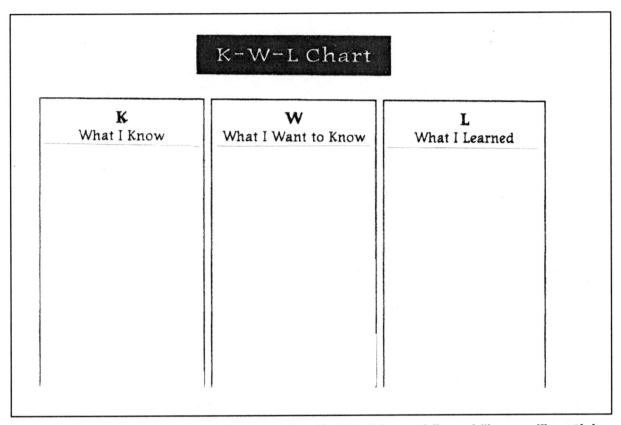

Figure 5.2: K-W-L charts can be used for "into", "through", and "beyond", activities in developing skills in content-area study.

Through Activities

• Oral Reading Strategies: buddy reading, cooperative reading, delegating good readers to read aloud, teacher reading

• Highlight important parts and key points in passage

• Make notes on post-its of important things to remember

• Verify predictions while reading

• Double Entry Journal: In the first column of a two-column paper, students write selected phrases, quotes, or information from the reading material. In the second column they write their reaction to the entry in the first column.

• Generate questions on the chapter for a "jeopardy" game

• Record passage on a tape and have children follow in book as they listen

Beyond Activities
• Complete third column of KWL, "What we Learned"

• Discuss What Was Read: Discussion can be with a group, with partners, or a whole class discussion. (The discussions should be directed by the teacher through the use of relevant questions or phrases.)

• Complete a special project: poster, choral reading, reader's theatre, music, etc. (Figure 5.3)

• Read a Related Novel: a historical novel or a novel suggested in the content area textbook.

• Play games to review the content

• Written Quiz or Test: Test can be teacher-developed or a unit or chapter test from the textbook.

• Create a class newspaper on the topic

Refer to the "Universal Access" section in Domain 1 to find strategies to provide for Differentiated Instruction to meet the needs of students with learning difficulties & disabilities, students who are English Language Learners, and advanced students.

Terminology for Comprehension

Character Analysis: Through a discussion of the traits, emotions, and reactions of the story characters

Evaluative Comprehension: An advanced level of comprehension which identifies bias, unsupported inferences, propaganda, faulty reasoning, fact & opinion, character analysis, use of language.

Genre: A term used to classify literary works such as novel, mystery, historical fiction, biography, short story, poem.

Graphic Organizer: A visual representation off facts and concepts from a text and their relationships within an organized frame. (example: K-W-L chart, Venn Diagram, Semantic mapping, clustering, Prediction chart, etc.)

Inferential Comprehension: A higher level of comprehension skills. Identifying inferred concepts such as main ideas, comparisons, cause/effect relationships; drawing conclusions, making generalizations, predicting outcomes

Informal Reading Inventory: (IRI) an entry-level assessment. Assesses a students sight-word vocabulary, oral reading fluency, and comprehension.

Informational Text and Materials: Materials with the primary purpose of giving information

EGYPTIAN SECRETS

Big Barter at Cairo Arena!

Yesterday at the Cairo Arena there was the biggest barter in Egypt. After the ships came in, more than 20,000 people rushed to see what they could find.

Included in the swap there was papyrus, animal skins, and clothes.

Next barter is on May 5. Don't forget to come.

More details on the next barter in Sunday's paper.

New Chariots

A new supply of chariots just came in after a long time with no protection. Now we are able to fight wars, no need to worry. Chariots will be available in two days. The chariots came from Babylonia.

Pyramid Robbed! No Suspects!

Last night a pyramid was robbed, and they still don't have any suspects. At around 7:30 p.m. last night the Cairo police showed up at Ramis' pyramid. Of the things robbed were jewelry, food, and gold.

A Crime

It's just been heard — there was a crime at King Tut's Palace. Someone stole his finest chariot. This startling event happened today at 1:00 p.m. We suspect they stole his vehicle because of the race that's coming up tomorrow. Now he'll have to use his second best chariot. They also suspect that King Tut's cousin is the "kidnapper". He will race against King Tut. The winner of the race will win the Pharaoh's eighteenth wife, and a few fold coins.

We think the cousin left the country until the race. The race is tomorrow at sunset.

A False Pyramid

Yesterday it was discovered that the new pyramid was fake! It was made of support poles and papyrus. When authorities went to check it out, a pole fell over and the pyramid fell down because the entrance blocked a pole.

When they told the Pharaoh he told them to find the builders. They could not find them. They must have started running right after it was finished.

It's hopeless! We will never find them.

Pyramid Robbed

At 5:30 a.m., a pyramid was robbed. The pyramid belonged to Seth, the evil Pharaoh. It is said that the robber was Fongo, the enemy of everyone. Please help us capture this crook. PLEASE.

King Tut's Camel Dies

After a grieving burial, with mourners and all, King Tut has vowed never to have a pet again.

The camel was practically murdered! In the middle of the night an arrow hit him in the heart.

This happend two days ago. The arrow hit the camel accidently. It came from two boys trying out their new bows and arrows.

The boys were sentenced to 30 hours community work — with no probation!

KING TUT'S LATE CAMEL

The Problem

One hundred years ago there was a legend. "The Sun Throne."

Every time someone stood up from the Sun Throne, the sky turned black and it became cold. When someone sat on it, it was sunny and warm.

Well, what are we doing to do? (- means to divide a word)

"Land of the Pharaohs"
A Project of Kellogg School GATE Program

Ellen Bablewski	Carli Foss	David Lappinga	Finn O'Shea	Nikole Villanuevo
Audra Baxter	Briana Heine	Elena Medina	Brandon Saiz	Meriza Viray
Jeffrey Birdsell	Jennifer Heine	Steven Millison	Stefani Saragosa	Heather Ziomek
Sarah Carmen	Katie Hutchison	Amanda Monk	Cindy Valladolid	
Juan Cervantes	Elena Ingoglia	Brendon O'Shea	Daniel Van Veen	

Advisors: Bonnie Johnston and Marilyn Dye   Principal: Robert E. French

Figure 5.3: Special project such as a class newspaper helps to reinforce the information and concepts learned in content-area study.

about a specific topic, event, or experience. Usually used in teaching the content areas – science, social studies, math, etc.

K-W-L: A graphic organizer outlining "what we know, what we want to know and what we learned"

Literal Comprehension: Explicitly stated main idea, details, sequence, cause & effect

Reading Comprehension: The ability to get meaning from text and to understand it from both a literal and an inferential level.

Venn Diagram: A graphic organizer to aid in the understanding of comparing and contrasting.

Thematic Word Wall: Words related to a theme or topic are displayed on a chart which is posted in the classroom.

Test Your Knowledge

1. Venn diagrams are visual organizers for understanding:
    a) narration
    b) causation
    c) comparison
    d) prediction

2. Graphic organizers are useful in teaching students
    a) effective study strategies
    b) how to organize information
    c) how to prepare for reading
    d) effective reading strategies

3. Prediction is a strategy for helping readers:
    a) understand their own world, as well as that of their peers
    b) understand the structure of the text, as well as the unfamiliar terms that may be included
    c) set a purpose for reading, as well as activate prior knowledge
    d) set a pace for reading, as well as a strategy for studying

4. Students in literature circles:
    a) prepare generic questions for future tests
    b) read and respond to good literature, engage in high-level thinking about books and do extensive and intensive reading
    c) figure out unfamiliar words
    d) help select books for the teacher for future use

5. A good teaching strategy to be used with English language learners is to:
    a) assign workbook pages
    b) present language skills in isolation
    c) use language as meaningful communication
    d) concentrate on sound-symbol relationships

6. Vocabulary development should be taught:
    a) at one time of the day
    b) throughout the day in all subject areas
    c) on computer games and worksheets
    d) b and c

1)c 2)b 3)c 4)b 5)c 6)b

Notes on Domain 5

For sample questions on Domain I got to www.rica.nesinc.com

Notes on Domain 5

Notes on Domain 5

Appendix

PHONOLOGICAL VOCABULARY REVIEW

Phonemes: smallest unit of sound represented with slashes /s/ /th/

Graphemes: written representation of sound using one or more letters
>   Example: the word "duck" has 3 phonemes, 4 graphemes

Morphemes: smallest meaningful part of a word
>   Inflected endings: s, ing, ed, ly, er, est
>   Derivational suffixes change the word meaning: less, ful, er
>   Compound Words: cowboy – both words have a meaning

Digraph: two letters / one sound
>   Example: ph, sh, ch, th, wh

Diphthong: two vowels, two sounds
>   Example: /oy/ in boy, oi in boil, /ou/ in house, /ow/ in how

Blends: two or three consonants that blend together
>   Example: bl in blend, str in street

Onsets: all letters up to the first vowel

Rimes: all letters following the vowel (including the vowel)

Phonemic awareness: awareness of sounds and ability to manipulate them orally

Phonics: phoneme-grapheme correspondence used for decoding and encoding (spelling)

Phonology: study of sounds in speech

Orthography: spelling patterns of written language

Etymology: origin of words

SUGGESTED STRATEGIES & ACTIVITIES

IMPROVING VOCABULARY
Sight words
- Word walls
- Picture dictionary
- Word banks
- Labels
- Word sorts
- Flash cards with high frequency words
- Repetition

Word Meaning
- Context clues
- Cloze procedure
- Building prior knowledge
- Synonyms / antonyms /homonyms
- Word wall
- Retelling
- Pictionary
- Morphology (root words/affixes)
- Dictionary
- Word webs

IMPROVING COMPREHENSION
- Story-mapping
- Sequencing
- Text structure
- Re-telling
- Re-reading
- Predicting
- Sentence strips
- Prior knowledge
- Visual /films/videos
- Cloze procedure
- Summarizing
- Questioning at different levels

IMPROVING FLUENCY
- Repetitive predictable books
- Read along with recorded stories
- Readers theatre
- Reading aloud daily at independent level
- Buddy reading
- Choral reading
- Echo reading
- Sight word recognition
- Cross-age reading
- Prosody: using diacritical markings for expression

IMPROVING DECODING AND WORD ATTACK SKILLS
- Syllabication: vowel generalizations (cvc, cvvc, cvce, & cv)
- Compound words
- Prefixes/suffixes/roots
- Building words
- Phonics patterns – onsets & rimes (word families)
- Blending/segmenting/ substituting sounds
- Shared & guided reading
- Direct instruction in: sounds & letters, blends & digraphs,
- Context clues
- Word sorts
- High frequency words

IMPROVING WRITING SKILLS
- Brainstorming – clusters, webs, etc.
- Journals
- Creative writing
- Pen pal activities
- Direct instruction in: Writing process, grammar skills, imagery, similes & metaphors
- Quick writes
- Class or individual books
- Vocabulary development
- Story maps/webs
- Using literature for models
- Author's chair
- Writer's workshop

IMPROVING ORAL LANGUAGE DEVELOPMENT
- Pair/share activities
- Show & tell
- Dramatization
- Group Discussions
- Story-Telling
- Language Play: rhymes, stories, alliteration, homomnyms, synomyms, antonyms
- Literature Circles
- Cooperative Groupings

DIFFERENTIATED INSTRUCTION
- Activate prior knowledge
- Scaffolding
- Vocabulary cards
- Writing/publishing personal books
- Daily reading
- Daily writing
- Realia – hands-on real objects
- Multicultural literature
- Primary language materials
- Cooperative learning
- Partner work/peer tutoring
- Work with bilingual aide
- Art
- Puppets
- Drama
- Songs, poems, choral readings, patterned text
- Teach other cultures
- Multi-culture Day with food, music, art, etc..
- Word banks
- Modify lessons – controlled vocabulary, speak slowly & clearly
- Model sills
- Share family traditions
- Preview/review
- Encouragement
- Storytelling
- Wordless books
- Graphic Organizers – KWL, maps & clusters, etc.
- Visual aids-films,overheads, maps, charts, pictures

- Bilingual labels around classroom
- Involve parents in school activities

IMPROVING ATTITUDE TOWARD READING & WRITING

- Interest and attitude surveys
- Shared reading with Big Books
- Guided reading activities
- Match student with books at their instructional reading level
- Co-authorship of books at home with parents or siblings
- Author visits/signings
- Author's chair
- Visit public library & get cards
- Write letters to favorite authors
- Incentives for reading – awards, parties, etc.
- Encouragement
- SSR/DEAR with teacher modeling
- Class library with a variety of genres & reading levels reflecting student interests
- Read-alouds
- Readers' Theatre
- Buddy reading or cross-age reading
- Book clubs or literature circles
- Author studies & thematic units
- Involve parents in student reading
- Book talks
- Turn off the TV
- Story maps for writing stories

IMPROVING CONTENT-AREA READING

- Build prior knowledge
- Skimming/scanning before reading
- Note-taking
- Clustering
- Graphic organizers
- Prediction/verification
- Preview/review
- Chapter Walk
- KWL
- Thematic word wall
- Videos
- Question generation

- Read related literature
- Projects-murals, timelines, class newspaper, posters, jeopardy game, special presentations related to topic or theme

ENCOURAGING INDEPENDENT READING

- SSR or DEAR time
- Reading materials at student's independent reading level
- Incentive: awards, parties, etc.
- Variety of reading materials related to students' interests
- Involve parents in students' reading

GLOSSARY OF TERMS

Academic Language: the language of literacy and books, tests, and formal writing.

Affix: A morpheme that changes either the meaning or the function of a root word.

Alphabetic Principle: The concept that each speech sound or phoneme of a language has its own distinctive graphic representation.

Anecdotal Records: written accounts of specific incidents in the classroom. The teacher records the incident, the time and place, and the possible implications.

Authentic Assessment: a measurement of performance on activities that reflect real-world experiences

Automaticity: Fast, accurate and effortless word identification at the single word level

Balanced Reading Program: A reading program which includes strong literature, language, and comprehension with a balance of oral and written skills, systematic, explicit instruction in phonics and decoding skills, on-going assessment, and an intervention program for "at-risk" students

Book Reports: Students read a book and write a summary, focusing on the main idea, character development, plot, problem, and resolution.

Checklist Assessment: an assessment form on which to record observations about specific skills development or behaviors

Choral Reading: Interpretive reading of a selection of text, usually poetry or songs, by a group of students

Cloze Procedure: a method for assessing reading comprehension by omitting selected words from a reading passage (usually every 5th or 6th word) and observing how many correct words the reader can supply.

Consonant Blend: Two consonants that blend together before or after a vowel. (example: bl, fr, st)

Consonant Digraph: Two consonants that make one sound. (example: sh, ch, ph)

Cooperative Grouping: Children work together in heterogeneous group of four or five students. In working with English Learners these strategies will help to develop their English proficiency and improve their learning

Criterion-Referenced Tests: Informal tests of specific skills or content and are designed to give scores in terms of specific performance standards.

Decodable Texts: Reading materials that provide practice in and reinforcement of specific decoding strategies.

Decoding: Strategies used to recognize and read an unfamiliar word

Differentiated Instruction: Instructional modifications or supplements to help all students reach their full potential, including students with disabilities, students with learning difficulties, English Language Learners, and advanced students.

Directionality: Concept that reading and writing in the English language goes from left-to-right and top-to-bottom

Echo Reading: teacher reads a phrase or sentence aloud and students read it back using proper rate, expression, and intonation as modeled by the teacher.

Emergent Reading: Pre-reading stage where students learn the concepts necessary to become a successful reader

Entry-Level Assessments: These assessments determine the level of students with meaningful indicators of reading and language arts skills. This should be administered prior to instruction.

Environmental Print: Print found in the environment such as on billboards, street signs, labels, etc.

Explicit Instruction: the instructional process - 1) Teacher models the skill or strategy, 2) teacher guides the student as they practice and apply the new skill, and 3) students work independently and give feedback to the teacher.

Flexible Grouping: students work in different kinds of groups with varied purposes, formats, and materials. Purposes for groups may be skill development or shared interest. Grouping should be flexible, with students moving in and out of groups as needs and interests change.

Formative Evaluation: gathering data during the time a program is being developed to guide the developmental process.

Encoding: Transferring oral language into written language. Students use their knowledge of sound-letter correspondence and phonics generalizations to spell a word.

Fluency: clear, easy, and quick written or spoken expression of ideas. Freedom from word-identification problems that might hinder comprehension

Genre: A term used to classify literary works such as novel, mystery, historical fiction, biography, short story, poem.

Graphic Organizer: a visual representation off facts and concepts from a text and their relationships within an organized frame. (example: K-W-L chart, Venn Diagram, Semantic mapping, clustering, Prediction chart, etc.)

Guided Reading: Teacher assists and instructs as children read in small groups

Guided Practice: A phase of instruction in which the teacher and students practice a strategy together after the teacher has taught and modeled the skill. The teacher gives feedback about students' attempts and gradually leads the students to independent practice.

High Frequency Words: Words which appear frequently in reading text

Holistic Assessment: Assesses a students ability to integrate separate skills into an entire selection. (for example; written expression, spelling and writing mechanics assessed as a whole)

Informal Assessment: Non-standardized, on-going assessment, usually teacher observation, portfolios, anecdotal records, conferences, etc.

Informal Reading Inventory (IRI): An informal entry-level assessment designed to help the teacher determine a child's frustration, instructional, and independent level of reading. An IRI includes 1) a sight word assessment, 2) an oral reading inventory, and 3) a comprehension assessment.

Independent Practice: The application of newly taught skills after skills have been explicitly taught and practiced under teacher direction.

Individualized Instruction: Students move at their own pace through self-selected or teacher-assigned materials with guidance and assistance by the teacher as needed

Informational Text and Materials: Materials with the primary purpose of giving information about a specific topic, event, or experience. Usually used in teaching the content areas – science, social studies, math, etc.

Inventive Spelling: a temporary stage of spelling in which the emergent writer attempts to spell a word phonetically when the spelling is unknown.

Irregular Sight Words: Words which do not necessarily follow the generally accepted rules of phonics. They should be recognized automatically on sight and read without hesitation.

Kid-Watching: direct or informal observation of a child in classroom situations

K-W-L Chart: A graphic organizer outlining "What we Know", "What we Want to Know", and "What we Learned".

Letter-Sound Correspondence: Concept that each letter has a corresponding sound

Levels of Reading:
> **Frustration Level:** a level of reading difficulty with which a student is unable to cope.
> **Instructional Level:** a level of reading at which a student, with the teacher's help, can read with understanding
> **Independent Level:** a level of reading difficulty at which a student can read and understand without assistance

Literature Circles: Students read a piece of literature and meet as a group to discuss it. The discussions are open-ended and focus on bringing the literature and the reader together. The group can respond to teacher prepared questions or can discuss reactions to the book - sharing favorite parts, raising questions about parts they did not understand or sharing their own reflections on the reading. The teacher monitors the literature circles as they discuss, and assesses the students' development, thinking processes and comprehension levels.

Literature Logs: After reading a section or chapter in a book, students write their reactions to the story in a journal, or literature log. These are written by the individual student to help them think through what they are reading.

Miscue: an error in oral reading

Miscue Analysis / Reading Miscue Inventory: an informal assessment that considers both the quality and quantity of miscues made by the reader

Modeling: The teacher helps the student understand reading material by providing examples. These might include "think-alouds", dialogue and responses, giving direct instruction, and providing examples of applying higher-order thinking skills.

Morpheme: Smallest meaningful unit of language - can be a root word or an affix.

Morphology: Study of the structure of words

Norm-Referenced Test: a test designed to report results in terms of the average results of a sample population

On-Going Assessment: As the teacher plans and instructs students it is necessary to monitor their progress on an on-going basis to determine if adequate progress is being made. Instruction should be modified as a result of these assessments.

Onset/Rime: Onset - sounds before the vowel; Rime - remainder of syllable. (example: c-at)

Orthography: the study of correct spelling according to established usage

Partner Talk: (Think-Pair-Share): Students exchange ideas by sharing their thoughts in pairs. Partners encourage each other and extend each other's thinking. Pairs take notes as they listen to the overview lesson. The teacher then has students think aloud and restate the overview lesson with their partner.

Performance Assessment: Demonstrates the student's competence in terms of an assigned response or product

Phoneme: Smallest unit of sound in speech (example:/b/ in big)

Phonemic Awareness: Understanding that speech is composed of a sequence of sounds and development of the ability to identify and manipulate these sounds. Not phonics

Phonemic Blending: Blending sounds together to make a word. (example /c/ /a/ /t/ = cat)

Phonemic Segmentation: Breaking words down to their smallest parts. (example cat = /c/- /a/- /t/)

Phonics: Systematic relationship existing between sounds and symbols and the application in decoding words.

Portfolio: a folder containing a collection of a child's work over a period of time

Portfolio Assessment: A portfolio is a type of on-going assessment. It is a collection of a student's work over a period of time. Contents of the portfolio should be dated. It should contain continuous samples of the student's work and should be aligned with curriculum and instruction.

Predictable, Repetitive Books: Books with controlled vocabulary which repeats words and phrase often and children can predict what the words will say.

Print-Rich Environment: an environment where a variety of printed materials are available, accessible, and used for everyday, authentic purposes. This might include color names, number names, labels, etc..

Prosody: the appropriate use of stress, intonation, and pauses in reading at the phrase, sentence, and text level

Reading Comprehension: the ability to get meaning from text and to understand it from both a literal and an inferential level

Reader's Theatre: Bringing stories and characters alive through interpretive reading of a script.

Re-Telling: An informal assessment of reading comprehension. The student retells a story or a selected passage that he has heard or read. Through retelling the teacher can learn much about a student's understanding of the reading passage.

Rimes: Words in which the "rime" (last part of the word beginning with the vowel) stays the same but the "onset" (part of word before the vowel) is changed. (example: cat - mat - flat).

Root Word: Basic word before affixes are added

Rubric: A rubric provides specific criteria for describing student performance at different levels of proficiency in different content areas. Students receive a number of points that represent minimal to high-quality work, depending on the type of response. Rubrics should have 3, 4, or 5 point scales, with the highest number representing the most desirable level.

Running Record: an oral reading assessment where a student's miscues are recorded by the teacher while the student reads a selection.

Scaffolding: Building on the student's prior knowledge. Begin with familiar concepts and build to more complex concepts.

Schema: Refers to how people process, store and retrieve information while reading. Pre-reading activities help to build on prior knowledge of student. Go from what the student already knows to new learning.

Semantic Mapping: A graphic organizer developed by writing a word or phrase representing a basic theme or concept. Students brainstorm words and phrases related to the theme or concept.

Shared Reading: Whole group instruction involving teacher modeling with whole class participation.

Sight Words: frequently used words (usually abstract such as the, see, and, said, etc.) that should be recognized instantly, without decoding or analyzing the components of the word.

Small Group Instruction: Teacher provides guided instruction in small groups to reinforce skills and concepts as needed. Groups are usually 5 - 8 students.

Sound Substitution: Changing individual letters to make new words. (cat - mat - mit - miss)

Standardized Test: a test, based on norms, for which reliability and validity can be verified

State Content Standards: An outline of mastery standards of the language arts program for each grade level, included in the Reading/Language Arts Framework for California Public Schools

Summative Assessment: indicates progress towards meeting mastery of grade level standards. Summative assessments would include quarterly, midyear, and end-of-the-year tests developed by the publisher or the school district.

Syllabication: Dividing words into syllables

Systematic Instruction: Planning instructing in a logical, sequential, and systematic format based on students' prior knowledge and progressing to a more complex context.

Teacher Observation: an informal on-going assessment in which teachers listen attentively and perceptively, during the course of each day. They evaluate as they listen and modify instruction as needed. Note-taking and record-keeping is an essential part of observation.

Thematic Word Wall: A Thematic word wall reinforces vocabulary words related to a theme or topic. The words are displayed on a chart that is posted in the classroom. Students or the teacher may add words to the chart each day as the topic is being studied.

Venn Diagram: A graphic organizer used to compare the similarities and differences in two objects or ideas.

Visual Aids: Using pictures, films, charts, posters, real objects (realia - manipulatives for visual demonstration), etc. to explain concepts

Vowel Generalizations: Generally accepted rules for dividing words into syllables

Whole Group Instruction: Direct, explicit instruction is provided for the class including modeling, building background knowledge, vocabulary development, guided practice, checking for understanding and re-teaching as needed.

Word Analysis: a process used to decode words. Word analysis skills include explicit instruction in phonics, syllabication, and word structure (prefixes, suffixes, compound words and root words).

Word Banks: Collection of known sight words students use on a daily basis. Words can come from names, labels, rhymes, patterns, dictated stories or experience charts.

Word Organizers: Brainstorming, mapping, and clustering or other graphic organizers which generate ideas about a given subject or text.

Word Recognition: Recognition and identification of the printed word

Word Sorts: Words sorted by consonant or vowel sounds, onsets and rimes, categories, concepts or themes

BIBLIOGRAPHY

Anderson-Cruz, H. & Saldana, J. (1999), *"RICA Written Examination Test Preparation Seminars."* (Based on the program advisory disseminated from the State Superintendent of Public Instruction and the California Department of Education, The California State Board of Education, and the California Commission on Teacher Credentialing)

Apgar, C. (1998, unpublished). *Preparing for the RICA.* (An unpublished study guide for the instruction of reading to pre-service students.)

Bear, D. (1996). *Words Their Way*, Upper Saddle River, NJ: Prentice-Hall.

Burns, Pl, Roe, B., & Ross, E. (1999). *Teaching Reading in Today's Elementary School*, Seventh Edition. Boston: Houghton Mifflin.

California Commission on Teacher Credentialing. (2000-2001). *Reading Instruction Competence Assessment registration Bulletin.* National Evaluation Systems, pp. 41-47

California Commission on Teacher Credentialing. (2009). *Reading Instruction Competence Assessment Registration Bulletin.* Pearson.

California Department of Education. (1999) *Reading/Language Arts Framework for California Public Schools*, Sacramento, CA: California Department of Education

California Department of Education. (2007) *Reading/Language Arts Framework for California Public Schools*, Sacramento, CA: California Department of Education

California Reading Program Advisory. (1997). *Guide to the California Reading Initiative*, 1996-1999. California State Board of Education, note from AB1086, p. 18

Comprehensive Reading Leadership Program. (1997). *Learning to Read.* Sacramento, CA: State Board of Education, Appendix A.

Cooper, D., (1997) *Literacy, Helping Children Construct Meaning.* Third Edition. Boston: Houghton-Mifflin

Cunningham, P. (2000) *Phonics They Use*, Third Edition, Boston: Addison-Wesley Longman.

Cunningham, P. (2009*) Phonics They Use*, Fifth Edition, Boston: Addison-Wesley Longman. Pearson Education, Inc.

Honig, B., Diamond, L., Gutlohn, L, (2000). *Teaching Reading Source Book for Kindergarten through Eighth Grade.* CORE, Arena Press, California

Johns, J. (1997) *Basic Reading Inventory.* Seventh Edition. Kendall/Hunt

Moats, L. (1997). *A Blueprint for Professional Development.* California State Board of Education, State Board of Education

Reading Program Advisory. (1996) *Teaching Reading: A Balanced, Comprehensive Approach*, Sacramento, CA: California Department of Education.

Rossi, J. & Schipper, B. (1999). *Case Studies in Preparation for the California Reading Competency Test*. Boston Allyn & Bacon

Ryder, R. , & Graves, M. (1998*). Reading and Learning in the Content Areas*. Second Edition. Upper Saddle River, NJ: Prentice-Hall.

San Diego County Schools. (1995). *"Everyone a Reader"* Tutoring Program. San Diego, San Diego County Office of Education

Templeton, S. (1997). *Teaching the Integrated Language Arts*., Second Edition. Boston: Houghton-Mifflin.

University of LaVerne. *Spelling Strategies* (based on Kottmeyer Spelling Series).

Walloon Institute. (1997). *Literature Circles*. A workshop based on ideas from Daniels, H. (1994). *Literature Circles: Voice and Choice in the Student-Centered Classroom*. York, ME: Stenhouse Publishers

Whistler, N, & Williams, J., (1991). *Literature and Cooperative Learning: Pathway to Literacy*. Literature Co-op, Sacramento.

Yopp, H. (1995). Adapted from *"Yopp-Singer Test of Phoneme Segmentation, Assessment Tool No. 5"*, from "The Reading Teacher;," vol. 29, No. 1.

CREDITS

Figure 1.1: Burns, P., Roe B, Ross E, *Teaching Reading in Today's Elementary Schools*. Copyright © 1999 by Houghton Mifflin Harcourt Publishing Company.

Figure 1.2: Used with permission of Marlene Giles, Valley Vista Elementary School, 2001

Figure 2.1: Rebel Williams, *Integrated Learning Workshops – The Balanced Reading Program*. Copyright © 1990 The Wright Group/McGraw-Hill.

Figure 2.2: Tompkins, G., *Literacy for the 21st Century*, 1997. Merrill Prentice Hall Pub. (provided by Russian psychologist, D.B. Elkonin, 1973.

Figure 4.1: Burns, P., Roe B., Ross E, *Teaching Reading in Today's Elementary Schools*. Copyright © 1999 by Houghton Mifflin Harcourt Publishing Company.

Figure 4.2: Hennings, D, *Communication in Action: Teaching Literature-Based Language Arts*, 1997. Houghton Mifflin Pub.

Figure 4.3: Cunningham, P., *Phonics They Use*, 2000. Addison-Wesley Educational Pub., Inc.

Figure 4.4: Used with permission of Robert French and Bonnie Johnston, Kellogg Performing Arts Elementary School, Chula Vista, CA 1994

Figure 5.1: Templeton, S, *Teaching the Integrated Language Arts*, 1999, Houghton Mifflin Pub.

Figure 5.3: Used with permission of Robert French and Bonnie Johnston, Kellogg Elementary School, Chula Vista, CA 1994

CPSIA information can be obtained at www.ICGtesting.com
Printed in the USA
LVOW090053140113

315553LV00001B/2/P